HOW TO

ANALYZE PEOPLE

Subtitle: the best guide to understand the deep art of body language. Includes tips about manipulation, personality types and human psychology.

Table of Contents

INTRODUCTION

Consider Both of These near-identical Situations; they begin with you sat in a desk of your favorite restaurant, it is a hectic night and you also fortunately got there in time to avoid needing to tilt the bus boy to bypass the point, and you are at the tail end of your primary route in deep conversation with your buddy about if to order supper or never. It is a cure nighttime, why not? So here is the waitress, she seems down in the desk and asks "are you finished using them?" Scenario one: she asks this question with her hands made into fists on her shoulders, stood up right her lips slightly pursed, and also the words from her mouth proceed fast without needing to see whether you're prepared to reply. Scenario 2: she's bent slightly to create eye contact, she begs for one to finish talking before inquiring her wrists wait her side or maybe even provide a mild brush off the shoulder, and she inquires with a gentle inflection in her voice since it's really a question rather than even a rhetorical gesture.

With No training and only from studying Both of these fictitious situations you're able to see what occurred and what these 2 waitresses were saying and indicating with their own bodies. In situation one of the marginally villainous waitress was actually saying "hurry up as someone else needs this dining particular table". In the scenario she desired you to leave but that she didn't need to make after all of you may need dessert, you feel pressured.

Nearly all people are capable of studying the principles of it, and Body language might appear mysterious and we have all at one stage let our body state things. Even without being conscious of this, you may understand that occasionally a meeting or trade goes really well and occasionally it goes horribly even with no subject of your dialog changing much whatsoever. The main reason why this occurs is you personally, or they've employed. You said the ideal thing by means of your face along with the individual reciprocated having a positive vibe, on the flip side, you could have experienced a stressful day and the other individual could see your aggression only in how you had been standing.

For a Lot of Us, body language that is flimsy might Cause real issues, occasionally we may seem angry when we're not, other instances folks may not take us seriously, or else they may think we're insincere. Oftentimes it's likewise crucial to pretend body language, in any moment or another we must market something (be it words, thoughts or used automobiles), and we all will not think in that which we're selling. We want our own body language to state we do. Fortunately, it's possible to alter how you utilize body language, also just being mindful of that hand gesture signifies what and exactly what the twitch your eyebrows may say, you should begin saying what you're feeling in either your body and words.

You will be educated How body language functions, what you're actually saying with your own body, and also the way to utilize your entire body, voice, and tone to state exactly what you mean. The publication will start by studying exactly what science could inform us about body language and the way it functions from the mind; following we'll research how our bodies function to inform us things, we'll then examine common body language errors, and ultimately, we'll examine strategies for successful communication with human language.

The Science of Body Language

As you have switched to this publication to Raise your own body language, therefore have associations and lots of companies turned into psychologists and scientists to learn body language functions and what makes people tick. Let's start with the question: what exactly is body language and try to find some use?

WHAT'S BODY LANGUAGE?

Body language is helpful as a source of Data, and a way to misuse. It may form part of persuasion and hands.

You've probably heard quotes such as "figure Language constitutes 55 percent of communication," before. Even though the amount,"55 percent," is really fairly useless, the concept stays evident that body language is also an significant part the way that people communicate with one another. Taking into consideration the reality that body language is critical, it is not surprising that everybody can read body language and also respond to this. On a sub-conscious degree, you may most likely already know whenever someone disagrees with what you're saying, or will be curious, or simply wishes to quit speaking to you completely. These cues are supposed to be known -- without that.

Body language is how we Communicate with all our own bodies. That definition might be misleading because normally body language isn't taken to comprise overt hand gestures such as the lifting of a thumb or middle finger, or using sign language -- these sorts of bodily expressions are at a sense still direct and verbal. Body language is usually regarded as the subtle casual or indirect facets of communication with our entire body, even only as little as a thumbs-up could be obtained as amusing given the ideal type of smirk. In reality some verbal communication is considered in precisely exactly the exact identical world as human anatomy as the way we say things is equally as significant as what we manner. There's a middle ground here naturally -- pointing out your finger is an immediate kind of communicating, but it could also be accidental and figuring out exactly what our hands do is unquestionably central to mastering human language.

Body language is your reading of the eye Moves, posture, facial expressions, and also the way we're going around to ascertain how to translate what we're saying, and also sometimes when we aren't talking, to translate exactly what a individual may be feeling or thinking. Its good not being anxious on your address with an interview, however if you're trembling just as if you are experiencing an earthquake folks will know that you are placing it all on.

The question of if body language is Accidental or intentional is a tough question. There are just a few rare chances to ruminate and observe what's occurring not just in the dialog but what's happening out and about you, answers happen nearly instinctually and you will frequently end up saying "that was not exactly what I meant to state", and also in these instances you may start to deconstruct your ideas to determine what you're thinking at the moment.

Our body language Appears to have less Input in our heads than that, that has resulted in a talking of a subconscious thoughts. This type of division is beneficial for plenty of inspirational speakers since it's striking and simplistic; the entire body is apparently acting on its rarity revealing your hidden wants -- restraining it could be a sort of concealed secret. The truth is that division is generally roasted with leftovers of Freudian psychology that's not obtained with much authenticity anymore.

For the sake of simplicity It's Ideal to Consider the brain as with the pieces you're presently paying attention , after which alongside this there's a whole lot of background information and procedures working behind the scenes but it is simple to focus on them and change or change them in your own will. A complete analogy is how a computer operates; normally you'd run only a couple of programs at one time. Certain individuals want you to believe your old mails and Solitaire are plotting something against you as you're distracted but that is not the situation. Body language functions within your conscious brain,. as whatever you're presently doing so, but it's also focusing on particular instinctual degrees and working with procedures that we don't fully comprehend - just yet!

We hear talk of just how much our Communicating boils into human language, a few characters indicate that 55 percent of what we state is found in the areas around our eyes and nose (one renowned figure implies just 7 percent of communication is language). When these figures change far from source to provide, and it is not always completely clear what these proportions even imply in actual terms, it is sufficient to be aware that a substantial number of routine communications is almost impossible without some kind of NVC (nonverbal communication). Contemplate how we speak with all text messages and internet chat programs; it may almost appear essential to work with smiley faces and emoticons because a lot of what we say could appear misleading or mad with no mouth or face to it. A very simple question like "Are you really coming into the dinner party?" Can seem accusatory. Consider also what we state is completely associated with circumstance, it isn't easy to even consider an expression which may be said beyond a circumstance. Simply take a very simple phrase such as "thank you", this may be considered dismissive, disingenuous, a pleasantry, or it might be considered something really pragmatic if followed by a kiss or rips.

We may intuitively feel the Strongest indicator of just how a person feels, following the words they talk, is expressed from their own face; nonetheless a recent research indicates this isn't the situation. The analysis indicates that people aren't brilliant at discovering subtleties of emotions in facial expressions and the amount of seriousness of an emotion can be very hard for individuals to correctly evaluate from confront alone. By simply estimating photographs of faces at a research performed at Princeton it had been demonstrated that without having the ability to check at the remaining part of the human body, individuals were just able to correctly translate an emotional condition 50 percent of their time. The more people understand about body language, the more people all understand how complex it is and the way each area of the human body is utilized. Body language -- stuff that is intriguing is not it?

Reading Body LANGUAGE

Thus, If the face is restricted in studying the Non-verbal grammatical signs of a individual, where if you look? The solution appears to be relatively easy: the toes.

Men and Women reflect their and their want By pointing their toes Focus. If you feel something away about a dialog, and find the feeling somebody would love to be someplace else, then glimpse at their toes and, even if they are pointing towards the doorway, there is your clincher.

Of Course, You do not need to spend your entire Time staring at the feet of someone. But take a peek and use their place to understand not or whether somebody wishes to maintain the dialogue. They are very inclined to be open minded to everything you are saying, if they are pointing at you.

It is if they are pointing away from you Possible you may also be speaking to a brick wall. The main reason behind that may change. It does not necessarily indicate you aren't liked by them; they have anything else in their mind or may be late for another appointment. You want to use your investigation that is heard and integrate body language to produce a comprehensive image.

Just How Much Can People Control Of The Own Body Language?

Our grasp and comprehension of body language Appears to be something and an inborn ability that's learned via experience. When you've spent plenty of time around infants you will know they can estimate from quite early on exactly what your face is expressing or saying. Tests performed on individuals blind from birth implies there are a few attributes of body language that are extraordinarily inherent, such as extravagant expressions like pumping both fists in the air whenever you're observing an occasion. In addition, we understand from the analysis of people who fight with NVC, like people diagnosed with glaucoma, our capacity to process information is essential to how we know body language. Tests performed at the University of Durham imply that individuals with disabilities could struggle to process visual motion fast, such as expecting directions individuals will proceed, and this ties in their capacity to fit up physiological movement together with all people's emotional states. There could possibly be an degree to which you cannot alter your ability to browse different people if your mind doesn't have the capability to process micro moves in different people and also to make predictions and determine patterns according to this info. But, it is apparent that teaching individuals to see body language in a higher degree is completed frequently and frequently so there's obviously some potential or capability to increase in this component of communicating. By way of instance, security forces are all trained by taking a look at their body language and attributes to identify characters.

In Regards to body language Can see in the way that it changes across the planet a fantastic deal of that which we know is directly taught or heard from the culture and people around us because we age. The intensity and length of eye contact fluctuates across the planet, in the USA it's crucial to supply routine eye contact, in certain Latin American nations prolonged eye contact may be regarded as a struggle, and also in certain Asian countries only short eye contact is viewed as polite. Something like a smile is not as it may seem it's a indication of happiness, others it's viewed as a kind of agreeableness. However, though these differences persist, it's probable you've got experience communicating with individuals from foreign nations, and you were able to do it pretty well: maybe without speaking a word of the language. Tests performed in the 1970s discovered that isolated tribes from the forests of Papua New Guinea could easily browse the faces of most Americans from photos with no understanding of American cultural standards.

What makes this even more tricky though, Is the body language does vary concerning area or nationality, but also job, within course, and from individual to individual. Everybody's body language is exceptional and the longer you spend with someone, the more you're able to read their own subtleties: if you have ever found yourself saying "why are you making that face" to your loved one, you understand exactly how particular their expressions could be.

Just like any Kind of language you create a Idiolect, and you also create methods of communicating with friends members and your loved ones that outsiders will fight to translate. That is basically inside stories, jokes, or keys that only those near you'd know. Consider how a mom understands that a particular sign from her kid means he needs his favorite toy, or the way a bunch of friends may have a ridiculous facial expression they find humorous which would look radically impolite to outsiders. There's enough common ground to create analyzing body language that a rewarding pursuit for nearly everyone, but remember that in case you would like to boost your own NVC on your work, you'll have to cater exactly what you find here to your surroundings. If, by way of instance, you handle a bunch of contractors, the language that they talk with their own bodies will differ compared to that of office employees.

Body language is more complicated than Don't be frightened although has been indicated! Not only does this vary based upon your culture, history, and history, but in addition, it varies depending on whom you're speaking about. You may find that you become Italian together with your hands when talking to a near-deaf Grandmother or you also embrace the back of a soldier if talking to someone you're drawn to.

Among the most important items About body language is it's to communicate a message. We make conclusions about someone, in their disposition, about their aims, in their interests and character nearly immediately: consider how it's possible to smell out a salesperson before they have even shown their true goals. We could make these decisions about someone, and the way they sense, from more than a glance; research imply it may take out as little as a minute up to a max of just thirty minutes, to achieve a determination about what's happening with somebody else.

These variables After all you could be Left believing much of my own body language could I control? You have come this way mostly residing in the present time, doing anything your own system has felt just like to express its own internal emotions, just how can you make modifications? The solution to this is really a combination of bad and good information. There's a sense where it's extremely tough to change the way you respond to your situation without a great deal of instruction and psychological reprogramming. It's possible to examine what all of the various gestures and facial quirks imply, however if you are mad it may be difficult to provide the impression you aren't. Section of applying body language is using a fantastic charge of your own emotions. Here is the significant trap frequently not shared with other people studying these kinds of novels, and that's that paying too much focus on body language may really make you worse in using it. Body language is so instinctive that focusing on this may toss it out of equilibrium, very similar to the way focusing on the way you're walking or breathing may make you forget just to get it done for a couple seconds.

There is hope, because There's an Connection between mind and the human body. Your system communicates what it is that you're feeling inside, however, your body may be forced to operate to this in reverse. Should you embrace the overall look of someone that's happy (by smiling or dance), or even the position of someone that's certain (simply by being relaxed and creating yourself big), then your brain will feel in exactly what your system is telling it and you'll begin to feel more happy or more convinced.

You can perform a experiment of grinning For 20 seconds, even if it's the greatest, worst, and many fake grin you've ever finished, you'll begin to see a change on your mood and beliefs. Should you really and do it correctly, you'll become aware of a much larger shift. Or you may try out the contrary, alter your physiology that it's in a condition or slumber whenever you're very tired, exhausted, or idle. Slump above, let back, body sink hangs, back and look back on the ground. You feel the changes and immediately can accomplish this.

Assessing your own body language, even a Functions at a positive feedback loop, bit. You get started flexing your muscles and you also truly really feel as a individual you get started acting like a person and your system starts doing of the Superman poses. There's substantial evidence indicating that your mindset can be shifted by adopting the position of a person to get a couple minutes. Because of this few psychologist really recommend violent or aggressive catharsis for a means of quieting down, and some fair reflection it makes sense: why would not beating a plate cause you to feel angry? Should you so learn the body language functions, and devote some time paying attention to everything you can are doing, then you are able to alter how others respond to you personally, and the way you're feeling about yourself.

It is likely to alter how you behave, Feel, by altering your behavior and act. As all of the components of driving an automobile come collectively as second character after you have been driving for some time, in order to embracing positive body language in response to distinct scenarios alter how we obviously act. By producing pathways: the longer you perform a specific activity, the faster and it could be carried out, your mind operates. It could possibly be that you'll have to clinic self-discipline, or perhaps turn into mindfulness meditation, to better manage yourself, but as soon as you start doing so permanent change will happen.

It's important to differentiate the way we can Read the way you respond to a circumstance and body language. We can quantify and examine how folks respond to pictures and situations and out of that we're able to acquire a fantastic picture of exactly what the typical American, and also typical individual, will do if they're happy, fearful, weak, stressed etc.. It would appear that if you can find out body language functions you may not have the ability to alter this, and may not be well worth researching. If you're a supervisor and everybody fears you since you're always mad, then it may indicate that you want to take anger management courses, since the issue doesn't lie on your own body language (it is just you are your own body is echoing the ideas of an upset individual), the issue is that you're inappropriately getting mad. On the other hand, the narrative given in the analysis of body language stipulates a picture that is higher.

Body language may make a demonstrable Chemical response in the body; what exactly does this imply? In tests performed with high density and low-power postures (high definition significance that you make yourself appear relaxed or big, and low-power significance that you make yourself seem little and shy), it was discovered that simply embracing a high standing posture may increase your testosterone, even though a weight-bearing posture could raise amounts of cortisol. Testosterone, when assessed by reduced levels of cortisol, is a hormone which compels you to take larger risks and also to project greater energy; cortisol is a hormone released when your system is under pressure so that specific kinds of bodily acts are placed to the back-burner so that your body is able to take care of the emergency at hand. In similar evaluations with different kinds of body language, like smiling, it was discovered that "happy chemicals", like melatonin, are published by simply acting happy. These aren't bogus responses in reaction to motions; they're bodily reactions which can make you happier or more worried, or tinier. You've got probably heard any of this earlier, but what's important to know this is you may change your behavior with focus and repetition, and this shifting of behavior is going to have an effect on the way you're feeling. On a lesser degree you might also learn to read body language to appraise unique conditions in your own daily life, which will permit you to get better approaches for connecting with individuals and for comprehending people sometimes at which you become blind into body language.

A word of warning or relaxation

Now you have a general idea today Language functions, what we mean when we discuss body language, and the way the analysis of body language helps us feel better about ourselves and speak more efficiently and develop better relationships with people around us. Before we delve into the way the body functions deeper it ought to be noted how it ought to be implemented, and that which you ought to take away from researching human body language. From the USA in particular a fascination is with emerging sharing the aspects of a salesman at all, extroverted and optimistic we do in existence. Whether we are attempting to receive our kid or dare I say, being a salesman or saleswoman and seeking to market something. A good deal of the conversation about body language is marketed as a method of shedding a more straightforward or meeker personality that's frequently thought to be a means of living: as a means of getting some sort of assured butterfly. It's necessary to keep in mind there are loud and silent methods of being strong, joyful, or positive and it's crucial to remember there's not any ideal method of doing things when you're speaking about communicating (no pun meant).

You Shouldn't Try to utilize body language To attempt to turn into a Hollywood picture of what there is a individual you need to attempt and turn into a model of who you're

In certain body language groups you may be educated to "fake it until you get it", or "fake it until you turn into it", therefore, as an instance, in case you need to provide a language you need to behave like a certain person in human speech, then you are going to grow to be a certain person in reality. You can't forget that building assurance is not as essential as having a motive to make sure, although That is excellent information. To adhere to the address case, it's important to work some superb content to your address, and to provide this address in a manner which works for your character. Becoming convinced can help you actualize this vision; however you shouldn't attempt and behave like a finger-snapping motivational speaker like Tony Robbins or even Les Brown if this is not how you'd naturally talk in public.

We could become spellbound Using things to do well we neglect to work with a CV that is great or workout exactly what we would like to communicate in the meeting. Confident body language would be the topic of a certain brain and you are able to use your understanding of your own body language to make the scenario, however, you can't really be confident in case you've got zero motive to be. At precisely exactly the exact identical time, you do not need to hold a panic that enhancing your comprehension of body language can probably cause you to fake, on the opposite, with more powerful body language abilities you'll make more and deeper fair relationships with individuals, and you'll have the ability to express yourself completely.

Talking Body

You will be Provided a tour of the human own body and every portion of it to men and women, communicates ideas or feelings to your own ears. It's possible to utilize this info to read people, but remember that men and women lie often without knowing this is being done by them, and it is possible that the expression may mean unique things. Tears are a classic example of a sort of body language which may mean things, although a individual may have nose and the exact identical cheeks.

When You're reading through this segment Attempt to think about how your body language functions and start taking notice of it and see how men and women behave. If You've Got Plenty of If you're laughing in a tv you need to make an effort and understand your own entire body in activity Show attempt to notice the way your face and torso are transferring. Seeing others, particularly if they're not being tired of being viewed and safeguarded, is Very beneficial to examine body language in scenarios and various situations.

Try to be more realistic About what could be accomplished together by body language. It may be that individuals show their Wrists when they're exposed, but they could only have wrists Not everybody is identical. It's best to not judge others Language if somebody is annoyed with you personally if you're able to stay away from it Face and shoulders, but they state they're not it's possible they're being "considerate". Enjoy what they are currently attempting to do and attempt to fix the origin of

Their aggravation as opposed to inducing a confrontation.

Types Of Body Language

There are different types of body Language it's worth beginning by just looking at how they can be broken down into ways that make them easier to understand. At the early part we discussed deliberate and unintentional gestures when communicating and we control. These terms will be used here on out to distinguish between the kinds of gestures we understand we are currently doing from those we might not be so mindful of. I could easily tell me I was deliberately pointing my finger in you personally, but I could struggle to detect that my foot bouncing up and down because it was being performed unintentionally. With this respect, casual gestures are things like crossed arms, head bobbing, biting your lip in deep concentration, or the way you could be sitting at a chair. These can of course be controlled things but we just wish to think of these as being 'outside' of command in a pure state when we are currently focusing on another event or activity. Body gestures can be regarded as three hands indicating three moments or an open hand telling us to stop: these are gestures which may readily be translated into words.

These gestures may be broken down further for closer examination. We've got release gestures that are often seen in things such as fidgeting or restless knees that are trying to discharge or relieve some kind of sensation, you frequently see people tapping their hands together when they're trying to remember. Another kind is that the micro gesture; those expressions can be quite difficult to see and will be subtle details and the moment. How an eyebrow is putting in your head or a little ripple of disappointment from the wrinkles around the eyes. Another different gesture is that the inviting gestures; those are gestures which are created very clearly to encourage what you are saying: that goes from clear gestures such as palms held aside to indicate dimensions or it might be overall hand waving to indicate intensity or passion. People stimulates neural pathways that are different or wave their hands because, in an odd way, it helps people think. This brings us to private preferences, these are gestures that a single individual are specific to that individual, or will possess. Personal gestures may be things like how a individual slicks their hair back when they're nervous. Among the trickier classes is imitation gestures, not all of gestures mean what they appear to mean, a grin could quite easily mean"please hurry up and leave" as easily as "I am happy you are here". The kind of gesture will be non-body gestures; that includes those you don't do, in addition to gestures that you do. For example, personal space is a significant gesture but it requires very little in the way of motion, other kinds of non-body gestures will be the way you are talking or perhaps what you could possibly be looking at.

- **The Feet, Posture and Legs**

We are currently going to Begin with your personal The items that keep you standing up and lead into your position and what it is saying on the planet, anchors. All these parts of the human body are in studying body language crucial as men and women not often control them. Aside from sometimes being advised to stand straight as a kid, people aren't quite aware how they ought to be standing or how they might guard their emotions by embracing a specific position, which can be more common with the hands and face. However, how we endure or where we position our legs states a lot, simply consider the how you naturally stand taller when you're wearing a uniform, suit, dress, or whenever you're in an important event. Should you look sunken and closed in it can even be an indication of a lack of sadness or control. Among the traditional signs of depression is folks walking much slower than they do.

When a physical appearance manifests itself In the posture of one, you know the person is usually experiencing a feeling that is strong. If someone has begun stomping the ground like a maniac, you're able to realize that as someone attempting to scare you or someone releasing built up tension or anger. Closely related to the gloomy slouch is your comfortable and joyful slouch. It's easy to spot the difference in the overall energy of the individual. When the shoulders are pushed back and the head is open then it is a sign someone. If you're currently trying hard to view their face then it's probable, they're sad. If you're feeling sad you are able to really go some way to turning it by intentionally breathing deep and gently, and seeking to break up your negativity by just focusing out of yourself as well as adopting a posture which opens your chest up to the world and which makes you stand taller.

Whether a person is just standing or Sitting can convey a good deal. Standing suggests someone is active and prepared to begin thinking or moving, you seldom start something lively by first sitting down. This is useful to recall if you're meeting someone and trying to earn a fantastic impression, if you are standing, you're open to playing about with personal space and touching, and it allows for increased use of strong body language that's unavailable if you are sitting down. Walking is a fantastic method of using the vibrancy of status and induces quick thinking in some and also puts another man at ease by preventing excessive eye contact. It is also an exceptional method of mirroring a different person, building connection, and sharing vitality as you need to commit to a similar pace to walk with another person.

Sitting is a standard condition in Life though you will have to know about what that portrays. It's simple to become overly relaxed when sitting which might demonstrate to others that you're tired or unenthusiastic, you might naturally do that by flopping your limbs about and twisting your head back again. If individuals are in this condition you may need to engage them first because they probably don't wish to be disturbed. Power poses frequently come into play when you're sitting the exact inward slouching is frequently a sign of sadness or powerlessness and something like massaging your neck works as a distraction and seems especially weak to other people. Contrarily, sitting up straight and spreading yourself out seems strong, frequently the more relaxed you even seem; the stronger you look. If you sit with knees crossed so that one foot is dangling in the air it may frequently be viewed as a thoughtful position in the right environment, it's used extensively by intellectuals and leaders such as Obama.

Whether sitting or standing, leaning towards Somebody is a good indication that you are interested, and also the reverse suggests you are not. Something such as a shrug can seem quite feeble and flippant, particularly if you are being dismissive or intentionally uncommunicative. However, like a lot of body language, just because something may appear deferential or weak doesn't mean it has no applications, a shrug may be friendly and open method of saying"I don't understand" and it allows someone else to feel comfortable accountable. The key is in the use of a joyful face and willingness to the shrug, thrown with palms open gesturing from the human body.

- **The Arms and Hands**

The hands are one of the most essential Tools you've got for communication; entire languages are composed of simply various hand gestures. Your arms can also be significant because they are able to attract people in, or construct a barrier around yourself. Your arms will be the organic object to use while protecting yourself, you naturally bring them around your face if threatened by a loud noise, and therefore people will see you as defensive if you adopt similar types of arm placements. Hugging yourself is clearly a indication of insecurity, and crossing your arms is something that ought to almost always be prevented because individuals find it a cold or perhaps competitive stance. Crossing your arms is frequently utilized to remain warm or as it's comfortable, but it could also show you are not ready to help out. One choice is the crossing of arms where your thumb is pointed up and the palms are slotted under the armpit, this can sometimes be a seen as a powerful pose, almost as though you're judging someone.

Learning to Prevent closure of your arms may Be quite difficult, especially if you are utilized to putting your hands in your pockets or even walking cross-armed. It may be useful to begin doing things, in a party hold a glass, when walking hold an umbrella, or when at a meeting possess a pen, but don't fidget. Wearing layers in sunlight is also helpful, it usually displays you're ready and also allows you to avoid having to shiver and heat up yourself.

Openness afterward, is your best way to approach Other people with your own arms. Opening your palms out before you show that you are open and don't have anything to hide. This is the place where the handshake derived, it wasn't merely a gesture of meeting somebody but was to demonstrate another party you were not carrying a knife behind your back. If you can, try to speak to the help of your hands, you don't need to start earning jazz hands but gentle miming of what you're saying with your palms is often well received by others. Be careful with your hands when they're at your side, avoid slouching and the appearance of these being dragged about if possible.

One of the ways to link with Someone (or ruin connection if performed badly) is with touching. In general, in areas such as Eastern nations and certain sections of Europe touching outside of a short handshake is prohibited territory with all but family and friends. You can include some components of touching to improve other common types of touching. With the handshake, By way of example a bit on the shoulder or closing in with another hand may create a connection of closeness. There's a lot of disagreement over challenging and limp handshakes, however in general a firm but friendly double-pump shake together using the webs of your hands feeling is fine.

One thing to consider when touching others Though is it will operate to assert your dominance, and this is not always a desired quality. Asking someone about the trunk following a handshake can seem very cold or corporate if it is in a relaxed atmosphere, or among people which aren't familiar with this way of posturing. That is the reason assessing the crowd is extremely important. The thing is that it come across like you are trying to create a relationship, and can seem computing.

It's best to avoid opting for touches when You are with someone and you are not certain how such a touch is going to be taken. Assessing the shoulder pat that is friendly with a colleague is something that you need to develop with time. You do not need to acquire a reputation for being "touchy-feely" and in some specific environments there may be legal consequences. Touching also implies a kind of leadership or dominance which might not be valued if you're trying to befriend someone.

Lastly let's consider the palms. The open Palm and wrists that are open is an obvious invitation theatrical styles may enter a space with arms and their palm wide open over their head. It may seem over the surface, but it is also instantly inviting. It may seem a competitive or domineering gesture Together with your palm down pointed like magician or a healer. Things to avoid would be the finger stage, and long hand rubbing: a fast tap or clap of the hands is great for producing excitement but don't go too far. Close your fingertips with each other, or interlocking them, often features an atmosphere of villainy around it, and holding your hands in front of you as in prayer will give a feeling of desperation.

When it comes to using your hands to Show things attempt to understand your audience, a great deal of hand slapping and clapping won't work for a shy or early-morning audience, but they can be successful energizers in a heated conversation. Signals like the "okay" 'O' along with your finger and thumb may seem a bit embarrassing, and thumbs up might appear childish or patronizing. Try to be practical and use your hands to convey your point, however, don't lose your character if you are a known hand-waver.

- **The Head**

The head is among the most important Because it is one of the centers of focus when we look at another person features. How we immediately get in touch with individuals is very phenomenal. A small experimentation you can do would be to take a look at a light when you're in a crowded place briefly so you have the imprint of light on your vision. Obviously be careful to not delve too long, but what you may discover by paying more attention to that mild imprint is that when looking at individuals you are drawn like a magnet to their eyes.

The mind itself is a significant area for Creating gestures, next to your hands it the major physical advantage you have for suggesting things. The state of your mind's droopiness is a sign of many things: when gloomy or contemplative you will arch down your throat and stare at the floor, looking upwards and eagle-eyed provides an awareness of power. Take looking up too much, or overly in-your-face along with your chin pointing up and others might believe you seem to be more arrogant. Thrust it even further forwards and your head becomes a weapon, even revealing people you're angry and dizzy. The extension of the neck suggests it may be quite a violent and intimidating gesture and you are focusing on a target.

Looking down and away can be a powerful Message of entry to individual or the speaker, it's dogs that are even worried and a look connected with kids. It is a gesture that is used much when you're being told away and is rarely a handy approach to interact with others unless it is used consciously and you are attempting to stroke their own ego. As individuals age, employing the head bow can nearly appear aggressive, signaling to the other person they are being overly harsh or that you are not likely to engage them on an equal degree.

Among the things that are powerful the head Will do is let off someone. A slight bow of an incline into the side or the head together with eyebrows that are broad can show disappointment. Should you intentionally avoid taking a look at someone when they're giving a suggestion it is also a powerful indication that you simply disagree with them. Turning away can be a method of putting a barrier between you and the other person; it can be aggressive or deferent to the other individual.

Head vibration is just another way you can Communicate ardently. Nodding up and down is always a way to answer to a question, but a small nod is a good means of telling someone you're paying attention. People that are meshing well bob together like toys in a car window. An extremely fast paced nod might be a sign you would like the speaker to rush up with what they are saying, or that you really agree. The head nod is also likely to faking, assess for actual engagement if you are not getting any verbal verification of what it is you're saying. Nodding your own head is a great way of emphasizing what you're saying; if you are giving directions then matching "do not use the fire escape except in a crisis" could be made stronger with a slight but obvious left and right head shake. People want to imitate you, therefore giving body language that they can mirror which reinforces an opinion is quite a tool that is strong to folks. Like any body language it might alter how you believe: you are well on your way to getting them to agree with you and Obtaining someone you've said.

A choice move of teachers is to give a Half "no" gesture with a quizzical look to the eyes. This is a soft method of telling somebody to fix themselves without even confronting them it implies you think they have the answer or you are waiting for them to get to a response you concur with. A mind throw is an obvious way of displaying anger to somebody; it can almost be cartoonish if followed closely by a sigh of disapproval along with a movie of baldness.

Nod or A quick whip of the head is an excellent Method of saying hello, it offers acknowledgement, but normally discourages long talk and is helpful if you've forgotten a title (you won't ever forget a name once you've obtained your free bonus following the end!) Or you. If you lean in to a permission it can have an almost "how can you really do?" Feel using a tip to it.

Curiosity and boredom are two types of Gestures that may be read from your mind. Propping up your head with your palms may say "I'd rather be asleep" when the eyes are either vacant or darting, or it may say "I'm enraptured by your every word" in case you're pushing up the chin for a better view, maybe even while taking notes of any sort to prevent you from looking at what you're writing.

- **The Face**

Attached to that mind of yours is your face and It's among the most fruitful and hard parts of the human body to see. Fruitful as it has many opportunities for viewing new items. Assessing your own face is also rather difficult, particularly if you're consciously trying to get it done. Often if you're attempting to seem interested or closed or impressed it's more effective to just start actually trying to become amazed: or even with the individual in hand then something else that is impressive.

Trying to corner every individual mechanic Of the face would have a long time so it's ideal to adhere with specific emotions and work them around. Always remember with all the face that there are lots of causes, what may seem like frustration that is ineffable could be constipation.

As it is sadness is difficult Not exhibited intentionally and lots of the aspects of sadness may also only be. Sadness is often accompanied by averting eyes indicating for you to not look at them, a hand supporting the head as though it may drop off, and the start of tears or heavy breathing, and the face in general enrolling a blank expression. There is little need to discuss significant sadness in the face since it's quite simple to read.

Anger shares a few similar notes, for Example there could be a blank face, but often the gritting of teeth is seen, overall anger may encourage the avoidance of eye contact but if it's concentrated at you, it's likely you can read it. Regularly pulling the face of a bull is a powerful indication that somebody is angry. Intentionally controlling the breathing is a indication that someone is fighting with their anger. Sadness, while stressed, is accompanied with a sagging mouth signaling a lack of hands.

A set of eyes fixed at you is An indication of management. Breaking eye contact is trying to leave a circumstance, it may say a lot of matters, and when someone is hiding an emotion such as sadness it could be a little cry for support. If you've got tight or cold lips it suggests aggravation or that you are holding back something. Being stressed is not necessarily a bad thing though. Should you just happen to observe a pout then someone is probably quite angry with you personally. Pursed lips may mean somebody is a bit annoyed, or perhaps just deep in thought; it's fantastic to look at the eyebrows -- when directed in the pursed lip is generally more inclined to be anger, nevertheless relaxed and empty eyebrows are likely to be caused by concentration.

Happiness is one of safest and the easiest Feelings to recognize: at least somebody is still happy if you get it wrong. The difference between a real and a fake smile is more difficult to spot, but only by making yourself laugh then giving a fake smile you can feel the gap in your face. Real smiles aren't often as intense or as toothy, and also ordinary smiles have been felt more in the jaw and at the rear of the throat. The eyes can also be crucial not or as you are able to see in a expression if a person is pleased. A fake grin may also lead to your eyes to squint more than naturally falling into place, since the muscles are being controlled rather. Don't look down too much onto a grin though because this reveals willingness.

Attraction may not be deemed an emotion By a few on its own but it's a significant element of studying a face-to-face and its particular most people want to know more about. Whenever someone is extremely interested in you something, their eyes will open wide, like they are an excited cat, the mind is going to be leant to someone and eye contact won't be forced or timid. Students may expand and if so there's definitely some sort of fascination, or signs of recent drug use. A lengthy gaze indicates fascination and if you've noticed has been produced. Some folks prefer to engage with a sly side glimpse which indicates you'll have to approach that person. A negative glance can be a sign they are not paying attention.

Repeatedly creating eye contact would be an Indication of attraction. Eye contact is for lots of people very important, a few studies demonstrate that it is essential for establishing fascination and trust in most western countries. Don't be too fast when it makes you uncomfortable to begin staring people down; looking nervous and nervous isn't necessarily preferable to uncaring. Blinking a lot is a sign of anxiety but reveals focus. People today struggle to tell the difference between real eye contact and somebody staring in a brow, so in the event that you believe you want to pay closer attention then don't hesitate to look there instead. A mouth can also reveal engagement with someone else. The kind of smile you have can be significant, if it is tight, slight or mild then it could be viewed as a gentle disappointed. Mouth that is and A jaw is rather a social smile asking others to laugh together with something. The negative glance is matched only by the side grin in terms of coy flirtation.

- **Assessing Others' Movements**

When You become more conscious of body movements If interacting with folks that are unique, and what they might represent, you should begin analyzing them. Everyone you come in contact uses their body to represent things that are various. Some folks are closed off, and many others may be open. These are some differences you can tell by observing a person's body language.

When studying yourself and others, it's important to try and behave naturally. It can be simple to turn into hyper-aware of your moves but know that you don't have to maintain your own body a specific way. As others might be, not everybody is conscious of body movements, hence at the day's end, do not start looking into your moves too much.

However, once you start studying others' body Moves, you'll start to understand it is possible to get to understand them. After meeting with a variety of people certain things may start to make sense. You speak might observe that one of your friends is quite pretentious in the way they hold themselves. Other buddies might reveal how insecure they are with themselves even though you thought they had been confident since they'd be known by you.

Knowing a Individual's body language and using As to why they might move a particular way, insight can allow you to understand them in their core. When it comes to persuading them, this gives you grip. You may want to match your boss' confidence if striking up a deal for a raise. You noticed you will need to become more relaxed around certain friends that appear to be nervous or timid. Becoming conscious of your body language could be scary at first, but you are going to be comfortable with the way that you move.

To Begin practicing being comfortable with Your own body, consider hanging out before a mirror. When you're eating dinner, perhaps lounging in bed, or watching TV, set up a mirror so that you can see how you hold yourself. You'll be able to see others proceed as well, once you receive an outsider's view on how you proceed.

- **Eye Contact**

Eye contact is among the biggest clues you Can use to ascertain how a person is. It is important because it gives clues about your nature and authentic nature to others, to become aware of your use of eye contact as well. Maintaining eye contact is crucial to let a person know that they have your whole attention and that you are interested in what they are saying.

It can be overused, however, and let Folks know that you are trying tough to convince them that you are listening. A lot of eye contact can occasionally intimidate others also, so you're having change it up every now and then if you find that a person is getting nervous because of the quantity of eye contact.

Pupil dilation can be a direct sign That there is a individual interested in exactly what you are saying. Studies have proven that if a individual's pupils start dilating whom you are making eye contact with, they are more interested in everything you have to say. They are listening to you with their utmost attention, and they're thinking profoundly about what you're saying. You know every time a individual's pupils are dilated while speaking that they are legitimately interested in the conversation.

The revise will be indicated by eyes. Someone who's considering your eyes back and forth is most hoping to convince you that they're listening. They are aware that they have to try and make eye contact, by what you are saying, however they are zoned out. People that have shifty eyes might also be lying to you or attempting to deceit you in some manner. They may be having trouble keeping eye contact because they know they're being deceitful.

- **Mouth Movements**

Exactly what someone does with their mouth is quite Crucial in realizing their personality. Someone using tight or pursed lips might be trying to focus, or else they also may be trying to conceal a face. You are able to analyze a individual's smile also. If the corners of their eyes are not creased, they may be forcing a grin with you.

Someone who is faking a smile isn't Necessarily bad too preoccupied to devote their full attention to what you are saying. Smiles can also be reactions to circumstances that are uncomfortable.

It's not because they when monkeys grin Since they're showing their teeth are joyful, but mostly. They'll start their mouths wide, showing they have teeth they could utilize to damage If they feel fearful and nervous. The same goes for dogs. When they are feeling threatened, they only reveal their teeth. For individuals, this is sometimes true but at a subconscious level.

Smiling and nervous laughing are just a way To get a individual. You can tell when they have creases in the corners of their eyes, somebody is really smiling.

A person that is constantly covering their Mouth also is usually nervous. They finger, might bite their lip, or put a fist Within their mouth. Understanding when a Individual is can Sometimes be helpful when seeking to persuade them.

- **Nodding**

How their head can tilt and turns Be a motion that is subtle. When they're moving their mind around the majority of the time are aware. The head and neck motions to will provide you great insight to.

Someone who nods their mind While listening to you may be anxious, attempting to move the dialogue. you talk 14, they are trying to set a rate. You are not talking, although they would like to allow you to know you hear you. Attempt to accelerate your words so as to maintain their attention if a person is doing this to you.

Somebody Who tilts their head May have a valid interest in what you are saying. They're trying to turn an ear, so that they could hear you, whether they are conscious of their moves or not. They are currently suggesting that they hear they and you would like you to continue talking. It is a means for them to get in the dialogue without needing to create interruptions or any interjections.

If someone is currently nodding too They might be trying to convince one that they are interested in what you're saying. They may have lost interest, although they might be conscious that they ought to be paying attention. In an effort to maintain, they feign to nod their mind. They may not realize what you're saying, therefore that they nod to create you believe that they're keeping up. If you discover others around, you're artificially nodding their mind, it would be well worth it to change the topic to regain focus or explain yourself as they could just be confounded.

Someone's head motions can be In using persuasion, very beneficial. A tip of their mind whilst may reveal that you're understanding what they are saying. Additionally, it may reveal that you are empathetic to them, particularly if they appear to be speaking about something which is difficult for them.

- **Hands and Arms**

Someone uses arms and their hands is You're interacting with. Our palms signify about ourselves. They are a method of expressing stories out, placing emphasis. They are likely to use hand gestures to keep folks interested, if a person's telling a story. Consider somebody engaged in a dialogue. They will raise their hands to keep up speed and a rhythm for all those.

The arms and hands of someone may express Shut or open they are. They can be into the body of someone. If they are crossed closely in front of somebody's torso, that individual may be a bit more shut off, not wanting to participate too much in dialog. Getting their arms crossed does not necessarily indicate that somebody is closed off. They may just need to break their armsso they listening to you if they hanging in the front of the chest.

Someone who gets their arms Above their mind, will be open and even attempting to exert power. Someone with their hands in their shoulders may also be attempting to maintain their power.

Signs

Everybody has body language ques That signs are used as by them. Using their own bodies may be signs that they are committing to the people around them, between genders, cultures, and ages movements someone makes. Signals allow individuals know pieces of information without needing to say anything.

A person with their arms crossed eyes Fading on a sofa at a party is providing the sign that they are likely prepared to go home for the evening. Someone else on this sofa may be sitting on the edge of the chair, laughing loudly, suggesting they are not likely to be heading to bed anytime soon.

The people are helped by signals round the signaler Know things they may not have the ability to communicate with their own bodies. Some are extremely good at picking up on other people's signs, and a few people struggle to know those around them.

When it comes to attempting to convince Somebody, there are a number of signals that a individual will have to be in a position to lead a dialogue.

BEGINNING A CONVERSATION

Next time you are sitting in a space Till they begin the dialogue to talk wait. This will let you study how they may begin a dialog. The majority of folks will give some type of sign they are just about to start speaking. They adjust their top, turn their mind, may clear their neck, or change in their chair. There's usually something, however little it may be, before they begin a dialog a person does.

When it comes to your turn Detect what you do before you start speaking, Dialog. Do not begin with an "um," or "uh." That lets the person know immediately that you are not sure of what you are going to state. Consider starting a dialog. See whether you're able to just begin moving your mind talking without clearing your neck, or doing something else. Study the way the other person responds. They may be amazed or thrown that you had begun talking.

Beginning a dialogue That's supposed to convince another individual, is essential for laying the groundwork to your debate. Nobody will need to give their entire attention to someone that's trying hard to begin. It is likely to be far more difficult to maintain if you are leaping through your words straight off the bat and nervous.

Leading The Conversation

When the dialogue has begun, it may Be tricky to keep the ideal amount of back and forth. You do not wish to be overly pushy, but you also don't wish to allow them to talk a great deal, not permitting you anytime to express your points. Should you feel as if another person is not letting you speak enough, you will find definite phrases you may use to talk your mind. You may try saying something like, "could I just say…,""can I talk for a moment?" Or "I am listening can I say something really fast?"

These Can Be Difficult to state in certain A few folks, and Scenarios could perceive you as being rude if you create a interjection. What your very best alternative might be to use your own body. Place your hands on your buttocks or tip your head to allow the person know you have something to say. Consider leaning in to tell them you wish to think about as the chief of your conversation.

The dialogue can be tricky, since nobody wants to follow somebody, they are being interrupted by that. It is still important that you receive your turn to talk. There are ways that if it's time to have a persuasion, it is possible to properly lead, that you can practice conversations. The next time do not. Let the person continue interject and talking. We get so apprehensive to state that our part we divert from the dialogue that is legitimate, invalidating we interrupted.

A different way to exercise the Conversation would be to talk the next time that you would like to state something. Force yourself to say exactly what you would like In case you have something to say but you'd keep silent. You will be given two views on leading a dialogue which you may not get by Both of these methods of training.

THE WAY YOUR OWN BODY LANGUAGE AFFECTS YOU

Believe it or not you use your body Can influence how you work. There are ways you could utilize to improve how you think, and also the ability of your memory by how you use arms and your hands. Not only are there any differences in regard to the way you use your entire body, however you'll also be affected by how you are perceived by others.

If you closed off There are a great deal of people who speak for you because they assume that you don't have any interest in dialog or may not open up. If you are always quite open with your entire body, exerting keeping and confidence yourself, others may wind up being intimidated by you. You may have no intention of shutting off others or becoming debilitating, but your body is able to demonstrate that in a way your mouth does not.

It can be tricky to become self-conscious of You can change what somebody thinks of you, as soon as you do, although Your own body moves. There are a number of people that may have a thought that is conscious, but they despise their entire body. Then they might close off others by attempting to conceal their bodies, which makes others believe they're judgmental. From time to time, there is a man or woman trying to cover up their entire body rather than themselves. You'd be amazed by how much confidence you may feel by simply changing up how that you hold your entire body. Folks can view what you look like in the event that you keep your arms . you are simply staying closed off, although you may think you are shifting other's perceptions of you.

Additional Ways That Your Body Actually Influence.

Open Your Mind

Someone that begins opening their arms They discuss will start to let others know they are a great deal. Should you reside with arms or simply hanging relaxed by your side, you allow the people around you understand that you're confident and prepared to converse together about different matters.

While having arms that are open is a sign for Other people, it is also a sign for your mind. Studies demonstrate that by standing with arms ones were crossed by; you can signal your mind. If you retained your arms crossed, you'll begin to think which you wouldn't. The same holds for the rest of the physique. The more open you're with your moves, the more you allow your mind to have thoughts that are distinct.

Boost Your Memory

The Ones That talk with their palms tend To get a greater memory. Using your palms can place physical reminders on mind for ideas and ideas that you may be talking about. Should you mimic shapes or numbers when you are referring to various ideas, particularly in a company setting, not only are you going to recall what you are talking better, but people around you may discover your story more memorable too.

Using your palms while telling a to speak Narrative will help you recall the things which you just went through. You are encouraging your mind to keep on believing, and maintaining your arms just as we mentioned in the previous segment, will start up your mind to new ideas and feelings you may not have experienced in case you have spoken with your arms crossed and shut off.

You have a Fantastic Summary of the Areas of the body function and the way they may indicate things that are unique, but in addition, there are lots of myths about body language and also lots. This segment dispels and will insure some of the ones. You are able to see a liar by taking a look at the dimensions of these students, from an excessive amount of eye contact, too little eye contact, or too much scoring.

The Reality Is that individuals are Excellent at lying with their voice and their own body: the perfect way to tell if somebody is lying to you or not would be to use standard reasoning. If you believe about the majority of the lies you tell it is clear this is the situation. Frequently you're currently lying about things or you've convinced yourself are somehow true.

On the other side, if you know someone And you've identified their 'informs', which can be activities or anchors if they lie, they perform, and then it is possible to use that as an indicator to ascertain whether they're lying. Everybody operates on customs and the majority of people have informs or anchors they perform if they lie, this might be as straightforward as sniffing their nose, tapping their hands on the desk, or massaging their chin.

POSSESSING BODY LANGUAGE THAT IS STRONG SIGNIFIES YOU HAVE ELECTRICITY

It can be tempting to believe like this However, the truth is you will work for people who don't project power but via subtler management of an area using self-belief and self-confidence. These folks will probably not carry themselves in stances that are feeble, but might not express gestures. Attempting to achieve power where it doesn't belong to you could end up with enemies being made by you or possess others feel as though you're overstepping your own mark.

GETTING INCONSISTENT WITH YOUR OWN BODY LANGUAGE

Among the most important items Body language is to be consistent in what you're saying with your body and what you're thinking on your mind. You may just lie , and whether you are attempting to fool someone, they might start to believe that this is true if you're portraying an excessive amount of assurance. Attempt to behave in character, although attempt to be consistent, folks do not need to feel you're unpredictable with your own body language.

Don't Be on the top

So you have learnt that which aspects of your own body Language communicate esteem and happiness? Do not begin trying to utilize them such as charms in a game. Body language has to be used naturally or others will believe that you're hiding something or you're only irritatingly happy or good-willed. Hand gestures should be used properly and shouldn't risk hitting different members of the face along with your principal goal with body language ought to be to fool yourself into using a specific emotion, not to tricking others which you think like that.

The statistic that was 7 percent was cited It comes in the 60-year-old study that comes out of a situation of communicating. In recent research there isn't anywhere near this kind of importance on what the body is able to inform different individuals, and other folks aren't that proficient at understanding others from body language independently. Before it was stated that you need to think about the way you speak with a individual that doesn't talk your language, and as you can normally get by, envision doing this with no props or circumstance and only solely using your physique. Charades would be a match if communication was everywhere near 93 percent of cues!

THE POWER OF THE BODY

Our bodies possess not just, and power with just how much we are ready to lift or carry. Strength is vital, but the weakest of individuals have the capability to control a space with their body movements. Now in the publication, you need to have a fundamental comprehension of what a individual's body language may imply.

We cannot get into each detail of the framework for how to test those movements is not there, although what someone activities may be attempting to communicate. As soon as you realize how someone else may use their own body to convince others, you may begin to work on your skills of persuasion.

It will not always work on everybody, although Their own body to convince other people to do exactly what they need. While some are repulsed by the notion Many people today respond to behavior. Others may be prepared for the struggle, although Many people today react from the ones that seem more powerful than them.

There are Lots of ways Which You Can use Your own body to convince others without being physically or sexual intimidating. Maintaining your body visible and open is vital in letting other people know they can trust you. Consider making sure to eliminate physical barriers which may keep you separated from the individual who you're talking to. Measure around table or a chair that is preventing you from making a connection you're wanting to speak to.

This shows that you are confident and Interested in talking your mind when hearing what another person must say. You may figure out what you can do to be confident when assessing people's moves. Study actors and find out how they maintain themselves. others may help you locate your footing in regards to getting a demeanor that is persuasive all around, although Everybody has their own moves.

Smiling is Vital

Our smiles are among the strongest Tools we have been given. Any situation can turn from poor to great just. Many people today feel like if they do not have straight teeth smiles which are glowing white, they are not worth anything. Even the ones who don't have their teeth may have considerably more amazing smiles than somebody who has spent tens of thousands on dental work.

A smile is showing. It is a means. Studies have shown that people will smile if they are smiled in by somebody. They will wind up having a mood, should they really do smile. Smiling can lift the spirits of someone, although it may seem strange. The next time you're feeling down, grin. It may do the job, although it seems absurd. Smile over and over again, and it will help to at least lift your spirits, though it may not turn around your mood.

The motive to learn about human anatomy Language is so you are able to communicate therefore a number of these dots will be linked so that you can see how to achieve this. Among the main things to realize is that others view you the way you view yourself: the crucial component to good communication is enhancing your disposition during positive body language. If it comes to utilizing our own bodies to convey you will find, however, ways we could be more proactive.

Rapport

The most Significant Part building a Connections with buddies, or Relationship with a individual that is new, is creating a rapport that is fantastic. It is since it's the aim of interactions, something which is talked about a great deal in body language circles. Whenever you're in great rapport you'll be reacting well to another individual's body language and you'll instantly need to be with one another, whether that's in a skilled or private capacity. How can you build rapport without ground or a spark? You do use a kind of body language called matching and mirroring.

Fitting and mirroring is what It seems like: it's you fitting the body language of some other individual so you instantly build a relationship and set them at ease. People today have a tendency to enjoy spending time with other people on a or using a mindset that is familiar. This will be obviously created by Getting your bodies. To do this you'll have to check at there is a individual behaving and acting, are they closed? Open? Can they talk slow or fast? What type of hand gestures are they currently employing? Attempt to look at what sort of body area they prefer and just how quickly they're breathing. You can attempt to replicate this. You should not attempt some sort of Groucho Marx mirroring, however only lightly adopt a similar position so you're as comfortable or on border as them, should they use large arm gestures then attempt to do exactly the same. Try and match the rate they're talking in addition to their quantity, don't attempt and match their emphasis but do avoid using fancy phrases if they're not utilizing them. By way of instance, if the other party uses the phrase intriguing, do not begin using glorious to describe exactly the identical thing, just utilize intriguing and it'll create the other party feel as though you're very similar to them. You'll realize that with doing so you can begin so they begin copying you following a brief quantity of 23, leading.

There are with here. If someone else is slouching and gloomy then copying may not assist them instead you need to adopt a similar position in order that they may begin behaving more like you, then open it up and attempt to smile. Equally if they seem to be competitive or antagonistic towards then you try not to replicate them but also avoid attempting to antagonize them by carrying the greater course with a more uplifting kind of human language. A fantastic understanding of body language ought to allow you to actually diffuse this type of situation by being composed rather than escalating or ingesting the anger of another.

It is necessary to Keep in Mind that Their own body is simply a part of the struggle. You do really have to have some material to what you're saying or they could be confused why somebody they're fighting to talk to is copying their every movement. If items are not natural attempt to come back to the individual.

The next time is exercised by A Fantastic For shopping, dinner, or even on the train. Look at other men and women that are speaking or simply individuals that are sitting alongside each other and may be strangers. You'll find the way they're in rapport concerning the positions of the arms and thighs, the speed and quantity in which they are talking, in addition to how when one party moves in a specific fashion, soon following another party will follow suit.

Folks create a error that is general when first Meeting somebody they try to construct rapport with their phrases by finding a frequent ground, just after this first rapport is constructed through verbal communication do folks then put in rapport to a nonverbal level. They key is to build rapport on a level through body language transition to construction rapport through communication.

Another exercise to try another out Time you're interacting with somebody, whether it's somebody who you've known for quite a very long time or just fulfilled. Notice the body language of each other and you'll notice maybe not or whether you're in rapport, normally some amount of attachment to a level will have already been established. If done so, you may start term it at matching and the mirroring. This signifies is that it is possible to move your leg or arm into a specific position or gesture and keep the dialogue, soon enough you'll observe that another party has moved in exactly the exact same gesture or position unconsciously. This is actually the power of rapport.

The mirror which can build rapport Is breathing in sync. This might be a good deal more difficult to perform in a business or social setting it's by far the subtle and most effective activity. This can be used for your own bedroom along with your significant other, check it out and thank me later! Breathing in sync does not only signify the exact same breath count but also where in the human body another individual is breathing, so are that they shallow breathing for their torso or heavy breathing all the way for their stomach. Are you currently breathing through their nose or mouth? Are they exhaling or inhaling?

Another Aspect is Everyone has different levels of comfortability based on how or near others are in dialog out of them. We are all aware that one individual who loves to put up in our face and nearly spit on us since they speak however, there are also other people that are more comfortable talking at a space where we could hardly reach them with our palms.

The next way of building Rapport is signature; attachment can be built by this than anything you say. This is more difficult to employ in a work situation however still possible; you might choose to book this for after until you are more inclined and comfortable implementing it into social settings.

If you are Want to concentrate more like tone of voice, speed, tempo, volume, language and key words obviously on the aspects.

Dating

Employing rapport is important at a date It's also crucial that you copy your spouse and don't reside on mind. Mirroring is used when something isn't moving well and you also notice you're out of sync physiological, but don't obviously take a look at their behavior and replicate each and every thing that they do. You need to attempt and be yourself you do not wish to devote time simply copying them. A link that is fantastic will ensure things move.

When on a date It's good to Search for Positive signs and continue on exactly the exact same route, but don't just repeat yourself or you face the danger of perplexing or alienating the individual when things feel as though they are moving. Among the riskiest variables in interpreting how a date will be that lots of the behaviors like being shy or playing with hair may be indications of displeasure and distress. You ought to have the ability to pick aside if these items are great are bad based on whether there is a power and joy to them and if they're geared at or away from you. As with language rules it's ideal to concentrate on yourself unless you are feeling a good deal of disconnection and after that you need to take actions watch and to mirror. Synchronization is natural so do not feel like if it is not, it must occur when folks are linking. It was not supposed to be if you're currently fighting to contact a person maybe.

Business Interviews

Fantastic practice in job and company meetings Interviews follows a good deal of the routines summarized here as good eye contact and preventing fidgeting or rubbing against your face. But, is a power play when in a meeting 17, to remember. You have to project confidence and power, but you want to stroke the ego of employer or your coworkers. It's quite great to embrace energy positions before going to the interview, even when walking to the construction maintain a fantastic position and when sitting take up more space than normal (without being obnoxious) and maintain an erect posture. Studies have proven that carrying energy presents for results are created by a couple of minutes at one time on a level with cortisol and testosterone. Results from bad and the latter poses, along with the former from electricity poses leading to confidence.

When You're in the area together with the Attorney (s) be sure to see how they're behaving. Many interviewers Really feel uneasy and they're happy for you to take charge Together with steer them and the discussions. This isn't Do not assume they're in charge and they don't although the case Desire you. Whether You Ought to mirror in this Circumstance Can be hard to judge since you would like to construct a level of rapport and You don't wish to seem cluttered or weak when they're powerful and However you do not need to announce if they don't, that you are equals Feel only, and that's yet the situation since they're relaxed doesn't mean you Must be.

The main Thing to remember is to maintain eye contact and face without beating the Person and to keep a great posture with your toes the flooring. Keep your breathing routine and allow your hands do a Great Deal of the Talking since they are not currently shaking like leaves in the end. Anything you Do, don't forget to keep a degree and to plan to your interview of body and charisma language during the interview.

WHAT IS MANIPULATION?

Manipulation Is a Sort of Impact That intends to alter others' behavior or perception via strategies that are indirect. By advancing the interests of this manipulator cost, these methods can be considered dull.

Social influence is not negative. By way of instance, people like family, friends and physicians, can attempt to convince to modify behavior's and customs. Social effect is regarded as harmless when it isn't unduly coercive, and impacts the right of those affected reject or to take this. Based upon the context and motives, manipulation may be constituted by social influence.

It of significance Definition of exploitation. Without there'll be an excellent deal of problem in separating other kinds of influence and instances of misuse.

While you have your own concept of exactly everything Counts as manipulation, so it's essential so as to generate sense of this guidance in subsequent chapters, that you adopt the book's definition.

Fundamental Ideas

Manipulation is your Attempt to impact perception or the behavior of the other people. Most definitions expand it to include "through the use of violent, misleading or otherwise exploitative means" or anything like a way of differentiating between exploitation and other affecting behavior's, like persuasion.

That raises questions, for example What represents "exploitative". Deception is simple to specify as modification or a concealment of this reality. However, does persuasion be actually precluded by deception?

In a job interview, then you won't Mention that the days you came to perform as a result of hangovers; would be that manipulation in your job? You might argue that anybody hiring for employment is working that folks are very most likely draw focus, and also to emphasize their positive characteristics. In that way, it is unethical to omit data . So anticipation may play a role in deciding the integrity of exploitation and in which the line will be drawn between misuse and other kinds of influence.

Placing aside integrity for today, there's A different word, because definition that is wide, worthy of focus. Discovering manipulation within an "campaign" indicates that manipulation remains manipulation irrespective of failure or success -- that the action of misuse is described as the effort. Paradoxically, those successful at manipulating other people, that are most often found, are more inclined to obtain a reputation as manipulative than people who triumph.

You can point to somebody on your Orbit, a comparative or co-worker possibly, that you believe to be more faulty. Think about how they are viewed by others. Are they known as a manipulator? Does their achievement is impacted by this? The reply to this, also, might be complex. If somebody is regarded by their peers in the office to become manipulative and holds influence over the supervisor, they may nevertheless be understood successful. It is very important to define objectives when considering others. This will let you earn logical, goal decisions, which can be essential to achievement.

Manipulation Vs Influence

The term has been embraced by the world Influencer for individuals who have a sizable social media after, effective at influencing others using their own content. It does not require a head that is critical to comprehend the origin of the term. As customer behavior evolves, advertisers have taken increasingly seem to exploit the energy of influencers to get attention for goods. This can be achieved through outstanding or paid sponsorships, arrangements and promotional prices.

In some cases, reveal these Arrangements while they do not. Ethical questions are raised, especially if a person influencer is apparently only a joyful customer however secretly on the payroll of this firm which sells this item.

Certainly, this entire moral quandary Might Have Been prevented, if advertisers alternatively coined the expression manipulator! Yet it is hardly surprising they did not. This highlight is that, though individuals expect advertisers to become manipulative, it's still unthinkable they would acknowledge to it. Instagram stars thankfully list themselves influencer in their own profile page with apparently no unwanted connotations.

However, the aims of influencers, especially people who operate with advertisers, are still essentially manipulative. It is not a grey-area matter. Influencers intention to change merchandise to their own followers so as to generate money. It's not feasible to understand if everybody they affect would gain from the item, nor can it be feasible to understand their financial circumstance or some other particular conditions. In cases like this, that the influencer is placing their interests.

Manipulation does not comprise an effort to hurt others. It needs to, to a level, set interests and your own objectives. This is a portion of the mystery.

Furthermore, It's safest and most plausible To refer to sway as a parent's period of exploitation; a single that includes manipulation along with other procedures of influence, for example inspiration and emulation.

Manipulation Vs Persuasion

These terms may appear In comparison, with persuasion behaving as the "honest" type of exploitation, in which the celebrity is up front in their targets and opinions. But for the purposes of the publication, it is going to be useful to think about persuasion for a grade below manipulation.

Persuasion becomes a Process of Manipulation, that is a type of influence. Persuasion also appears to be among the procedures of misuse. How frequently have you ever been in a disagreement with somebody else, just to allow them to maintain their hands and say "I wholeheartedly, you're definitely correct"? It's most likely possible that you rely on these cases on a single hand.

It may be Simple to convince someone that Smoking is poor but is it effortless to convince them to stop? Authorities would not find the need or advantage in putting taxes so as to discourage usage if it had been so. In accordance with the definition of the book, the government utilizing a variety of approaches to attain that end and is currently hoping to control the use of tobacco.

What about other types of sway? And Procedures of exploitation? Well, manipulation ought to get intent and it should have some sort of target if this aim is to make anarchy. It's obviously different from manipulation although A filmmaker may help determine the function of others. The filmmaker does not set out to affect others (even though they might), instead they attain influence throughout the response of the other people to their job, leading to inspiration and maybe even emulation.

Persuasion isn't the sole Method of exploitation you can use. A kind of disturbance is still lying, be considered and to lie will alter the perception. It's still manipulation whether it's effective or not, as has been demonstrated.

Persuasion, for example sway, does not suffer From the exact identical picture problem as exploitation. In reality it is regarded as a positive point to have the ability to generate a "persuasive debate " Even though it does possess a sinister tinge; the term "that I can be quite persuasive" suggests some effort of power on another celebration -- maybe an insult. Additionally, when companies refer to this delicate ability of "persuasion," it's right to comprehend that as a euphemism for exploitation.

Defining Manipulation

It is possible to make a and Definition for the aims of the publication of exploitation.

Manipulation is a form of willful Influence, characterized as an effort, by a individual or party (that the manipulator), to alter the behavior of some other individual or party (the goal), normally having a view to attaining a target from the manipulator's interests.

There's no response that is nefarious, nor will be It stated whether the manipulator is currently behaving in against, or without a respect for the interests of this goal. All are potential. This accomplishes a definition of exploitation that's not restricted by thoughts that are ethical that are abstract. Although that does not mean that you should leave your morals!

This definition is useful as it's Clear and objective. It is helpful since, within this publication, you will learn. It could be an error to exclude persuasion, that can be inextricable from the hints inside this publication and can play an essential part.

Two issues remain, nevertheless. The first Relates to "planned impact" Intent is difficult as it implies duty. Everybody manipulates everyone about all the time, even. It'd be incorrect to exclude a child's temper tantrum in manipulation's umbrella as they aren't mature enough to reevaluate their behavior. The same is applicable to temper tantrums that are grownup, for this issue. Intent doesn't indicate behavior. This also allows for its, quite real, existence of "obviously manipulative" men.

The difficulty is that the disappointingly Vague end: "generally to attain a target from the manipulator's interests" Not only can it be problematic to specify "that the manipulator's interests, but" there's a catch-all ambiguity from the addition of "generally" This component wouldn't match a definition and serves only to make a notion of exploitation. All things considered; how can somebody know their particular interests? It's obviously possible to control somebody, and for the result.

Cases of Manipulation

Together with the definition It's now Of use to comprehend a few examples of manipulation. A number of them are common in everyday life, but some relate to occasions that are particular or spectacular. Although this novel relates to manipulation, there's not much gap between manipulation within a grand scale and in a individual level. The principles always employ but also the practicalities of like deception, exploitation procedures, may be complex between, state, warring states.

Advertising

The most benign advertising is Attempting to notify you personally, with a view to altering understanding or behavior. It's, by the definition of this book, manipulation. Some advertisements might have positive goals, like adverts to raise cash for charities (even though the moral practices of charities may and also have been drawn to question on several events) or even a positive effect, including an ad which informs you of real savings or benefits extended by means of a good or provider.

On this scale, your end Have advertising techniques such as influencers, who try by supporting emulation of the lifestyle to influence your decisions. Additionally, there are online ads that are frequently indistinguishable from many other articles -- even the very moral sites generally just flag up compensated advertisements using a little "sponsored" label; additional times, ads might be wholly undisclosed.

By highlighting Promotion can control The qualities of service or a product. It's hard since they are biased to trust adverts. Techniques like subliminal advertisements go to extremes to induce messages about a merchandise. That is only the tip of the ice hockey -- block, although you might have seen examples of messages or figures squeezed to market alcohol.

Military Strategy

History provides examples of . Like in advertisements, this exploitation is expected. In the event you think in the reason for which you're fighting, it's also morally justifiable to control your enemy at all.

The Battle of Hastings (1066 AD) saw the Norman William the Conqueror (spoiler alert) attack England with all his army, comprised of mounted knights. Harold Godwinson, the King of all England near the English Channel, in Hastings satisfied him. According to legend, the Harold waited for the invaders and took place. William, viewing the drawback of battling ordered a retreat, with the aim of enticing the defenders. The strategy has been a success. Sensing success, Harold forfeited their position chased the military of William and, in the process. The rest, they say, is history: William's set knights could conquer the mostly infantry-based military of Harold and his success thwarted his only major resistance in England.

Even Though the accuracy of the account has Been called in to question, this legend's lesson prevails: control your enemy and success will be achieved by you.

You can find cases of wars Fought as characterizations of leaders. Rommel, a German WWII overall, was famous for his strategic genius in North African campaigns from allied forces, making his nickname "the Desert Fox."

Methods distort or to block the data obtained, with a military adversary.

It is likely to draw on parallels to Games like real time and chess approach video games, even where plans revolve round deceiving your competitors with respect to your intentions.

The Professional World

It is Very Likely that if you operate in a Business You have been subjected to people whose objective is to scale the ladder. In the world, a degree of exploitation is to be anticipated. This is only one reason that working with private friends can cause complications, even as a battle is present in handling these two distinct sorts of connections -- aggressive and supportive.

You are introduced with a selection of dating paradigms that are various. Your connection to staff members will change to people working under you, or to this along with your supervisor. Modern structures are usually flatter than it was, as well as is not as workable. It is up to supervisors and team-leaders to "inspire" their workers. If you identified inspiration as another kind of 12, Nicely done.

Personal Relationships

This is the most contentious Stadium for exploitation, yet ironically it is the most ordinary. From the minute that you're born, you are back with the capability to shout -- a straightforward and productive method to communicate immediate wants, so as to get attention and care.

Manipulation occurs in household Relationships in addition to in relationships and friendships.

The reason for controversy is suspended from the Is suspended in a demand for management and something abnormal. Although there's some area. It is fairly normal for a parent to control a child's behavior using a system of punishments and incentives. That is regarded as a portion of growth and a part of a child's schooling.

Manipulation at a connection, nevertheless, Is seen as something less than pleased. It frees up the notion of a person blackmailing their spouse in traps somebody or order disguise behaviour in a connection and lying. On the opposing side of this coin, it is plausible that individuals would commend manipulation, such as deceit; when the end goal was to aid a spouse quit smoking or shed weight.

These questions are all addressed In the publication. For the time being, it is just helpful where manipulation could be current, to take into account scenarios. Consider analyzing the world to see examples of exploitation where they function, and comprehend the mechanisms.

Benefits of Manipulation

The Advantages of exploitation are Evident, similar to the advantages of bank robbery. Manipulating others is a means bend it to your will and to affect the world. That may sound menacing, but remember it is extremely probable that you are doing this to a degree.

To distinguish between what you may Be doing and what you're able to learn from this novel interpret this chapter because the advantages of knowingly, manipulating other people and intentionally.

- ### **Achieve Your Objectives**

By manipulating you, other people Can change their perspectives, their behavior and potential their aims to help enhance your interests. It is as straightforward as that.

Successful manipulation is all about Enhancing your speed of success. It may be that everybody is manipulating your boss, to a level, so as to find that advertising -- but just 1 candidate will have the job. Working hard will be a fantastic place and functioning is better. Making it to merit may not get you. Do you create it so your boss would like to encourage you, as opposed to anyone else? Knowing that will provide the advantage to you.

It's 1 thing You enjoy them, yet the next to be the object of the desire. Successful manipulation is all about cultivating a circumstance where your achievement is the most probable (or the inevitable) outcome.

- ### **Help Others**

You are able to encourage if You Think in an effect By utilizing manipulation to enhance its own success it. This may be anything from having a jar to prevent a cursing that is comparative, to assistance for your party.

It is Just like achieving your goals But you are minding the interests of something or somebody else. Exploitation is a sort of influence, as mentioned in the definition.

- ### **Guard Yourself contrary to the temptations Others**

The more you know about exploitation, The better equipped you will be to prevent being manipulated by other people. Recognizing hurtful behaviors in different men and women won't just defend you against their sway, but you are going to find out more about their own objectives, feeding your head with details which you may use to control them.

It is Not Difficult to be Conscious of scenarios Where you can expect to experience behavior that is manipulative. What is harder is to identify the manners in.

An Integral part of the knows the aims of Parties and they're trying to attain those goals. With this advice, not only are you able to understand and capitalize upon others' behavior, it is possible to develop the capability to forecast the activities of your adversaries.

Intelligence is required by this, since it Is vital to have the ability to put yourself. In creating this skill, a fantastic place to begin is by learning how to understand your decisions and checking your behavior. After chapters will insure that in certain detail, although doing this will need some training.

Manipulation Fundamentals

It's time A number of the facets of manipulating other people. As a result of this phases, you must have the preparation develop an overall comprehension of strategies and to provide context.

Goal

Your Goal.

Provided that you are probably Being exploited yourself, and Assessing the people around one to a level, define and the very first step in attaining manipulation would be to comprehend your goals. Without aims, it is not possible to assess the efficacy of your manipulation attempts.

That is not to say that you are Manipulating with some amount of strength. Some of us are more manipulative and a few individuals are manipulators.

Begin by considering your activities Your behavior around other people. Think about that you see, and who you see favorably, or on your circle. Consider, moreover, if it contrasts to your view of those and the best way to act around individuals that are different. There's a great probability it does not. Actually, what you are likely doing is currently working to make the opinion of other people that you think to maintain sway and power.

This is a general strategy that Society is taken in by Everybody. Your behavior all around your boss is different to that of your coworkers, irrespective, to use an instance.

You Might Even have a group goal Reaching" position. You could be attempting to impress. You may even be attempting to split a simple work-life for yourself, losing accountability and doing everything you can to obscure your reduced productivity. You're behaving to make yourself closer into some co-worker in whom you are interested.

All these are merely ideas. At the conclusion of every Day, consider your behavior. What do you really spend attempting to realize and considering? These are the targets you are currently working towards. You may surprise yourself when you understand what your reasons are.

To Be Able to Begin manipulating It is time to knowingly and definitely define your objectives. That is fantastic if you have already done so. Ensure you've got something using a defined ending point. As Opposed to simply "do well in the office," believe "make an increase," or, Better Still, "make a salary of $X Each Year by MM/DD/YY." By establishing a target A date you're giving yourself the motivation of preventing failure.

You can begin Assessing your activities. Ask yourself "does this activity help me attain X" And also you may have the ability to make decisions. Do not stop reading yet! There are a number of factors until your behavior abruptly changes to make.

The goal of Others

While your aims are the method the achievement of your campaigns, others' aims are crucial to forming a manipulation plan that is successful.

The aims are being used by the Trick to manipulation Of others.

This really is the theory of The heart of the book and manipulation's method of manipulation.

Occasionally, the cards might be held by you also may Help a person to realize their objectives. This could be as a worker who owns resources for the boss to accomplish success. It could be the situation that you're the boss and also have the capability to market folks... not ignoring the energy you need to help those folks today reach their aims by not shooting them.

Having everything it takes to assist Individuals Achieve their aims gives value to you.

Here are some examples of scenarios in That your aims might interact with people of the other, to be able to gain you

Sticking with the area Reference, state that among your co-workers is placed to some trade expo in charge of a company trip. No matter their career goals might be at the point, it's very likely that a part of attaining them is to have a trade expo.

If that Individual has reason Assets will enable them to attain that victory, they're very most likely to take you. Will be beneficial placing you in position to get a promotion and possibly raising your worth.

That is a simplified example This particular point of thinking. It appears clear, however, it is possible to generate an appraisal of where you can fit into the aims somebody wishes to attain by breaking down it.

It May be your company Is to attain profits, strategies to enlarge your branch. They may choose to do so based on your division's accomplishment or the development of an enlarged market for the support you supply. The effect could be an increased demand for the labor -- suddenly you have become in value and it could be more difficult for the boss to deny offering a raise to you.

By Way of Example, state that you operate in a new technology, along with Construction business enters the end, which appears to need crane performance and you also happen to be an experienced crane operator. In cases like this, your manager is currently seeking to employ crane operators, that requires time necessitates other and training investments in their own role. It is very likely that giving a boost to you, your supervisor could prevent cost of hiring a brand new the hassle.

In Both These examples, you've got the Capability reach their objectives. That is exactly what pushes your success. There's not any element of exploitation here -- it is an investigation of your goals could relate to all those others. The manipulation will include cultivating these circumstances align to your own.

Now, think about relationships. Imagine that you are interested in somebody else. Your goal may be to enter into a connection with this individual. All the sudden, things become complex.

Not only is it uncertain what a Individual might Want for you in the connection, it may be uncertain. A lot of individuals haven't considered exactly what forms based on the attraction. Therefore, in the event that you would like to control the situation to end in the beginning of your relationship it might be crucial that you recognize that person.

<u>For today, simply hold onto the thought as a Thinking purpose.</u>

Actions

Having said activities, It is acceptable to give a paragraph. Actions are. Their behavior is defined by the activities of someone. In identifying routines activities could be realized. An act could be anything in a facial expression, or even body motion that is involuntary, to conclusions and address in addition to acts of sabotage or violence.

Tools

Understanding goals supplies the necessary For manipulating other people Advice. Tools, on the other hand, would be the materials which you need in your disposal to impacting those aims.

Power

Aims, in the last segment, you browse a few Examples having to do with the office regarding situations in reach their objectives. This translates into electricity.

<u>Power is the capacity to assist Men and Women succeed.</u>

This is a fascinating definition because It seems to subvert the notion of electricity as a ability to apply pressure. Breaking down it both are related. Possessing the capability to exert pressure over others may mean not damaging them not invading their nation, not throwing them into prison, not producing legislation which negatively affect them these are all kinds of energy -- the capability to help other men and women succeed is substantially like the capability to make different men and women neglect, abandoned unexercised.

<u>These are negative and positive Views of the thing. The distinction is negligible.</u>

What can you supply Their objectives are achieved by folks? The issue that is clearest is abilities. Talent is invaluable in each facet of daily life, to company, from sports contests. That is a thing, In case you have abilities which folks may use.

Another sort of electricity is jurisdiction. The Boss has to choose who's fired and who's promoted. You can be arrested by A police officer or let you away due to their jurisdiction that is sanctioned, with a caution. A judge can determine their view of your character, and your sentence, dependent on limitations.

There's a problem Exactly the higher, or same, talents as yet the other person. And they appreciate gains that are greater and might be more effective than you.

Another facet to electricity is standing. This is related to the view on your own power. Its standing that is crucial to manipulation. The decision of the other people seeing your own ability, along with your skill.

Persuasion

One is persuasion. Recognized it as an instrument inside the umbrella of exploitation, and having analyzed persuasion in connection with manipulation, it's currently worth analyzing its own usage and creating a definition of persuasion.

Persuasion is the attempt Their activities to modify.
The Issue with persuasion is that, It is clear to the individual which you have an incentive. They think that you stand to profit in the courthouse, which can be unhelpful when attempting to control a neutral or friendly celebration, and catastrophic when seeking to control an equal.

Persuasion is helpful when you can Show information to alter others' perception. has an opportunity of succeeding, if somebody is very likely to modify their path according to new information or new understandings of advice, which you may supply. This usually means providing advice which will influence the aims of a different party.

The other situation is if another Party considers your goals have a connection with their very own. In cases like this, they just also take up your cause, and also can trust your decision, along with your goals.

That is great if you have fresh Advice, or the hope of some other individual. However, you won't ever. On these occasions, when coupled with persuasion is going to be more effective Additional tools, like deception. That means trying to convince someone on fact or even a lie. You are showing major or new information Someone to think that your targets align with theirs, but in fact you're currently generating or hiding components.

Subliminal Persuasion

The Concept of persuasion involves Convincing somebody to do something. If you are being picky concerning it you would persuade someone. You might attempt to convince them to get without them realizing what you are doing everything you need.

The Concept of persuasion is Thought of advertising. There are companies that can do anything they can to convince people to purchase something, even when it means bothers us. Subliminal persuasion's concept does not need to be insidious.

There are many parts of subliminally Persuading a person. You need to ensure you're doing this. You do not wish to become. It is not about tricking them and getting in their mind. You utilizing this into your strategy for persuasion and ought to be considering everything you understand about these.

It is not about Manipulation

You never want to make Someone feel like They are mad. You do not wish to offer. Subliminal persuasion should only be utilized as a wonderful way to tell someone how you truly feel as if you may be too frightened to say that the obvious truth.

Some people have a more difficult time Accepting reality, persuasion, or fact than many others. These sorts of people cannot be told what somebody needs. People prefer to disagree only. There are ways around asking somebody you may take.

Persuasion Should Not be about manipulation. You should not be "tricking" somebody into something which is only going to help you. You ought to use this procedure from becoming independently persuaded avoid and better to try. Additionally, it is valuable for obstinate, intimidating, or other varieties of people who cannot be easily conversed with.

Confidence is Essential

The key to subliminally persuading Somebody will be always to exude as much assurance. There are a few people who will observe confidence and that means you don't need to carry it too much. But nobody will be convinced, however subliminal you're getting, by somebody that cannot even stand up to their ideas and opinions.

Confidence is important to be able to Distract the individual from recognizing that you may be attempting to convince them of something. Picture speaking to your mother or dad, expecting for to borrow the car back if you're a teen. You'd want to utilize some assurance, but not too much that you'd like them to believe you do not care about their own consent. So as to subliminally convince them, you could bring the reality that there is nobody else that will safely induce you to a celebration. Rather than intentionally asking and providing them the choice to say no, rather, you are more able to influence them for the kind of believing. It may become their concept to allow you to borrow the car for the weekend.

Body Language Approaches

Body language notions that are Separate were Discussed, providing you insight to somebody uses their own body which they do. Utilizing these very exact techniques can also be important if it has to do with subliminal persuasion. You will want to demonstrate confidence, while also keeping vulnerability, even when seeking to subliminally convince a person.

Maintain Speech Clear

An important part of persuasion Is to really talk clearly about what you would like. Some folks can be duped if you talk fast or utilize confusing words they don't know. This is not fair and could be a kind of abuse that is negative.

Rather than attempting to fool somebody into You can certainly do it. Plan out everything you need to state if you have to, but not overly much. You do not need to have the dialog to feel just as if you are being overly formal. Rather, pick out a couple of important factors you feel are needed, in addition to some essential words you need to place emphasis on in your address.

If someone can see that you're talking With diction and optimism, they will be more inclined to agree with everything you are inquiring than if you simply fool them into saying yes by employing confusing and jumbled terminology. In that way if something goes wrong after the deal has been made, it is possible to remind them that you simply put out the conditions quite clearly until they consented.

Framing Conversations

Like we It can be unbelievably beneficial to set out the frame for those conversations which you will be needing with other folks. You don't ever wish to write down just what you're likely to say, since this can come off really static and clearly practiced. Nobody would like to respond or state "yes" compassionately into a robot.

Framing is significant because it helps construct the base of your own instincts. You will want to write down exactly what your objectives are, and the way you are going to start achieving these. Additionally, it is important to incorporate the lumps and affects you may face so that you can prepare for all people too.

Pick Positivity

It can be Difficult to remain optimistic, particularly when seeking to convince someone of something severe. Positivity always works much better than utilizing negativity. Frame your orders utilizing words as opposed to ones that are negative. In case you need to ask your visitors to borrow $1,000, it could be nerve-wracking. Rather than utilizing a negative excuse, including, "I only lost my job and I am behind on all of my bills and do not understand how I will catch up," attempt being positive, including, "I just need $1000 since I am in between projects, but that I applied to a few new places and also understand that the $1,000 is I want to be sure I do not get behind"

While the two scenarios are catchy, your Parents will find they will not have as much danger with the next phrasing they may face from the very first situation. It is the exact identical circumstance. You are unemployed and you require cash. But you discovered that the positivity from the next phrasing, revealing your parents that the hopefulness of this situation also. That is important in more ways than simply asking someone for the money.

Get people to begin saying more. Rather Of asking somebody, "When are we likely to specify a date to your wedding?" Consider asking, "How can November first seem?" Rather than giving the choice to dismiss the dialogue to them, they must face the problem head-on. Do not give someone the choice. Think of a yes, no question which it is possible to request that could begin directing the dialogue.

Another example is requesting your Members to really have a celebration. You would not wish to state, "Could I have a party tomorrow?" This provides the choice to them. Instead, consider ,"How about we have a party tomorrow night and then Sunday we could spend all day relaxing and cleaning " This sets the concept of the image in their mind so that they're more inclined to say yes, so rather than making a notion is confronted by them they may wish to say.

Plan Your Outcome

When it is always advisable to Consider the start, the center, and also the conclusion, by writing the publication prior to going on. By doing this, you may contain items at first which may result in hints. How frequently have you watched a film, just to realize that there were indications to who the murderer was!

This Type of preparation is very essential to have In some specific discussions. You may consist of hints, if it's possible to plan exactly what you would like to obtain from a particular interaction. This is a significant method to prime in addition to put the frame for.

Physical Persuasion

You look could be quite Persuasive for someone else. Not everybody is big, so they may feel like they cannot endure to other people. It may be hard to be a person that must stand up!

Larger may feel as they have trouble. They may feel like all folks today see is that their own dimension, perhaps not giving them an opportunity believing they may be too hard or intend to strategy.

There are ways about our physical Look which could help convince men and women. They could have connections not centered around fear if a person is big. The ones that are somewhat far smaller than can possess a voice.

Selecting What to Wear

As much may not like to acknowledge it, It may be important that which we decide to utilize when creating discussions. In selecting what's right to utilize the initial step would be to ensure it's something. This does mean something which contrasts with your style and clothes which you would be observed in, although sweatpants. Others may tell if you may not be sporting something you would. A lawsuit may seem as a costume on somebody that in slacks and tops.

The next step is to Make Certain That it The event is matched by appropriately. Many folks wish to have dressed up believing their jewels and threads that are best can make them seem. So you can be approachable you wish to be certain that you're not tripping it.

Designs and color are significant to Consider. Warm colors could be tempting, but a thing that is too daring of a color of red or yellowish may also be a sign to be careful for another individual. Green and blue may be welcoming colors but you do not wish to seem just like the ice hockey king in baby that is an excessive amount of. Someone reacts to a color might be an immediate indicator of how they will react to your persuasion.

Scent is Vital

Scent is more persuasive than most Individuals would believe. There are a few department stores which release so as to evoke a more happy mood which will make people to spend cash Christmas smelling aromas!

When it is important to Wear something, which fits with your body odor. The samples you watch in the shop for cologne are not so it is possible to smell the item, just. Additionally, it is so that you are able to try out the scent out and find out how it blends. Perfume can be costly but consider it like an investment involving persuasion instead of only something which will make you smell pleasant.

Deception

This is just another tool for exploitation. It Forms the heart of ways to manipulation and also with persuasion and electricity significantly.

Deception is the control of information.
It and start thinking objectively becomes Possible to envision people. The machines have been made to reach targets, and certainly can do this by responding to inputs

(data) and generating outputs (activities). Should the input signal are controlled by you, simply by controlling that info, you are able to fool. With this disturbance, the sparks are able to alter, leading to actions.

The Reason Why deception takes a function that is fundamental In manipulation that you manipulate to think their actions are furthering their own interests. They don't have a motive. Deception's aim would be to control data in which direct them.

Of Course, the threat, together with deception, Has been discovered. Deception is avoided where possible and also, when employed, to be controlled. If discovered an deception could have minimum risk and maximum benefit, together with plausible deniability. There's also the danger that lies may lead to additional lies, so as to pay up the initial disturbance; in this circumstance, the danger dissipates while the payoff stays the exact same and what may have looked like a fantastic idea initially can turn into a terrible choice.

Irrational Behavior

Thus Far, in the principles of There has been a premise based on the thought that parties behave. That is a fantastic assumption. What might look like behavior is a case of somebody having objectives.

It's of interest, to a Manipulation attempts, to estimate the rationality of anybody's goals. Even though the volatility (accountability to alter) of these targets is of attention, the rationality of these isn't. The issue that is main is to ascertain a individual's goals through their activities and use those aims to forecast, and control, their activities.

By Way of Example, a co-worker may be slacking Away on the job. They may not be doing all of those things necessary create a fantastic impression or to accomplish a marketing. Is their behavior irrational? In the event you presume their aim is to progress their career, although it might appear so. Actually, they concentrated on chasing a love interest, or might be on the lookout for a simple ride. They may be more enthusiastic about their own life beyond work and just opt to make some respite during business hours, so that they could bash it up all night . In that way, their activities aren't absurd. Is that aim logical? It matters.

Behavior is really a collapse that is cognitive To perform activities which help attain the goals of one.

The Individual in the previous instance might Have a aim. That does not mean that their intentions align. They could be called their own objectives if a person isn't actively acting to realize their objectives. The behavior is not irrational.

Behavior is similar to a sign of The brain. It's a mistake, based on too little comprehension or a failure of intuition. This differs from a scarcity of information, where someone is able to still earn a mistake, nevertheless it's rational behavior dependent on the information available for them.

A Fantastic example of behavior is Enjoying with the lottery. Men and women play for the opportunity, although Everybody understands it is that your ticket will probably triumph. Something about intuition motivates individuals to gamble to get a benefit.

The Identical strategy is used by media Programs, that have found an endlessly scrolling is the means to tap into a twitch of intuition. Folks today scroll down down on the page, showing new articles and articles, every time betting on if something is going to be of curiosity or more drivel. It plays to the exact identical risk/reward mechanics like the lottery, and manipulating human impulse to secure more advertising views, maintain individuals utilizing the programs for more and boost their earnings.

Not everyone is vulnerable to those Methods others of exploitation. The way behavior fits to manipulation to the book's approach is just as a portion of behavior that is observed. It does not indicate it is arbitrary, because behavior is absurd. In realizing a individual or party That makes it as easy as behavior.

<u>The Main Thing is to Know about the Chance of behavior, work it and identify it.</u>

Manifestations of Manipulation

Strategies to manipulation are manners of Using to impact others' activities. To employing a team, to manipulating a range of individuals it may range from manipulating a individual.

More, you certainly Doing this. Examine a number of the strategies and think about how they may relate to a own daily life.

Emotional Manipulation

This is not distinct from the lettuce Of manipulating individuals, As well as the stick entails intelligence.

You will find a Number of ways in which individuals Manipulate others. All these, in some sense, work above to impact another's activities. It may seem natural to conclude that psychological manipulation's aim would be to excite behavior. Abuse is more inclined to distort the facts, via a shift in fact, to the extent that somebody's changes their way to realize their objectives.

Analyze an approach The guilt trip was known as by Manipulation. The guilt trip entails attempting to make somebody feel much worse about an activity they've obtained (or an activity they've neglected to carry, which amounts to exactly the identical thing i.e. sitting and not tidying your area is an activity).

You are currently trying To influence their reaction. The yield is for this individual. So they may either, You're changing their understanding of a circumstance: make amends to their mistake or fix their behavior.

Here's a breakdown of those mechanisms:

They're worried with their loss of reputation. The end outcome is going to be a reduction of electricity, should they create a reputation as somebody who can't or won't assist other people to reach their objectives. By making amends solving the matter is really a means.

They are being persuaded by you of the severity of Their mistake. As mentioned before, neglecting negativity, this takes one to offer real new info, like a previously unknown unfavorable effect of their mistake -- possibly a fiscal cost to your self or another -- or even have enough of the hope they think that the view of view of occasions to be legitimate, making them reassess their very own.

Of Course, You can use deception to Fabricate the aforementioned -- formulating. A good example might be lying around an accident they caused somebody unintentionally, playing its seriousness up. This may be an effective short-term strategy at the same time that you'll be discovered finally.

Is Influenced by your own electricity. They're inclined to be submissive for your requirements, in case you've got the capability to fix the issue they've caused. Your power would be the capability to help them attain their objective of conserving their standing and that raises, the larger they perceive their mistake.

Tripping is far from the sole type of Psychological manipulation. It's hard to draw the line between manipulation that is unethical and moral. By way of instance, what represents guilt tripping as opposed to expressing disappointment? They are the same. What is the distinction between intimidations?

There are conditions for different Kinds of manipulation. It's not required all of these, or perhaps understand, to memorize. By knowing the mechanisms of manipulation that is psychological, you are able to examine and understand these as they appear. Listed below are a Couple of examples:

Intimidation -- Provoking dread in a goal, such That They Might change their Strategy for attaining their objectives. Specifically, intimidation that conveys a danger of violence may promote a goal to modify their course of actions in making sure their particular self-preservation (a rather universal target). Acting to support their intimidator becomes their own behavior, also is a method for the goal to endure.

Notice That There's nothing absurd in the target's behavior here. Abuse isn't always absurd behavior's provocation. Bonus points if you understood this is barely distinct from the "stick"

Seduction -- Manipulating a goal by introducing them with an item of Withholding it, and Want performs an act.

The thing could possibly be another advantage or the seducer, like cash. By seducing the goal scam emails from Nigerian princes operate.

Seduction Could Include Provoking Foolish behavior. An alternate method of seeing this is because a persuasion to control others' aims, putting a sexual experience.

As it's, seduction revolves around electricity Presenting and persuading the capability to provide. Bonus points if you understood this is barely distinct from the "carrot"

Minimization -- Here will be the attempt to Decrease Somebody's view of a problem, . It might involve any manipulation instruments to decrease the size of the matter.

It involves persuasion and Deception, emphasizing or generating details to demonstrate that the absence of significance. Additionally, it may demand rationalization, which will be currently describing the causes of the activities of one to justify them.

Though this bears no connection to Power, see how individuals respond to the behavior from somebody who has sensed power, in comparison it.

Blaming -- Death the blame for a mistake onto Somebody Else is a method to by safeguarding your standing, utilizing disturbance or persuasion Conserve your energy.

Notice how easy it becomes to crack down Actions, such as attributing, employing these 3 tools.

In Addition to passing the attribute, creating Blame may be a smokescreen that is handy. Blaming a sufferer is a method of persuading a sufferer so as to control a individual that is vulnerable, that their standing is under danger.

Now, you may realize that Blaming is connected to intimidation. There's the danger of harm to someone's reputation, which may change their activities or harm.

Charisma

It's difficult, although not impossible, to Learn allure. Since it retains ability, But, it's still vital to mention charm within this publication.

Charisma is the illusion of electricity. Along with the Illusion of electricity is strong.

Envision a individual that is charismatic. You are Probably considering a speaker, that let an anecdote, also will hold an audience. What's deception, or persuasion, if no one really pays attention? Charisma dictates a lot of what's known as magnetism.

And there are individuals in places of Appear to be charismatic. CEOs, actors and politicians are all charismatic amounts but you will find several dozen fumbling.

Charisma is not everything but it may get You quite a way. It is possible to seem to have significance by producing the illusion of energy. It still stays powerful the same Even though, deep down, everybody knows that charm is an illusion. behavior coincides with how gifted men and women are predicted to act. And it is probably there's some significance to this.

It is safe to split appeal into Two component parts, every pretty useless without another:

Confidence -- Confidence is also a natural consequence of proficiency, which can be a natural Result of expertise and skill. It follows that, to seem confident will provide the impression you have both, or even both, natural capability and expertise i.e. useful traits that could assist others attain their objectives.

Wit -- Wit will be your capacity to think fast, in your own toes. It's the Equivalent to your brain of a somersault. Agility is demonstrated by it, giving proof of your skills that are exceptional and comprehension. Better yet if you are funny.

Imagine all those traits other. Who's very likely to generate a fool of these witless idiot, than the usual bragging? Without humor, is poised to expose themselves.

Useless is that the genius that is quiet. The In case you have not obtained the confidence most witty comment on earth is not likely to improve anybody's perception of your energy.

It is likely to work in your charm by Enhancing your confidence which means accumulating developing and understanding abilities. Attempt watching men and women talk that is charismatic, see the way they make and what type of comments they create positive responses. You need to observe that men and women seem to find it more easy to link to a viewer -- a indication of intelligence. Chapters in this publication cover assessing others and you may use those abilities to come up with your charm.

Charisma Isn't necessary for exploitation, However, it delivers a shortcut.

Human Psychology

You do not need to become a psychology specialist to Possess a simple understanding of how the mind functions. You can start to examine people As soon as you get to understand how our brains function. You'll begin to understand that people may behave a particular way due to the way and what they have been educated. You will begin to assemble the bits of what causes the folks around one of the unique people, when you've got a fundamental understanding of psychology. You will realize a whole good deal more makes sense regarding a man does the things.

Even people in person Psychology make errors. There's so little known naturally, not everybody will be correct all of the time. The mind is the most complicated organ in the body of any creature, not just people. It can be tough to comprehend it and determine what secrets lie within that make someone tick. You are still able to try to get to understand a individual's brain's inner workings, and you will begin to know them somewhat better though you wont have the answers.

There's little known regarding the individual What's understood, and Mind was discovered from the mind! Is not it odd to believe our brains taught to us what we know more about the mind? That is part of the pleasure of attempting to find somebody, although this organ will not make sense to anybody.

It is important not to use someone Psyche contrary to them. The intention shouldn't be to convince folks to do something by. Some individuals have. Others do not have what is needed to understand that they may be taking advantage of, though some people choose to stay ignorant. You shouldn't ever knowingly take advantage.

Some People Today require Strategy, mostly as they aren't prepared to face their own troubles. Not everybody has a fundamental comprehension of their mind or it believes and can what exactly it will. Some folks are scared of their very own heads, so that they are prepared to face their feelings as individuals may be. It is important to stay patient with people who may not be as you possibly can.

WHAT'S HUMAN BEHAVIOR?

According to a definition;" behavior can Be described as the actions or responses of a individual in response to internal or external stimulation situation." To understand a person's behavior we must comprehend what that individual will do if something else occurs.

Approving or disapproving behavior is As evaluating behavior known. A lot people appraise others according to their activities and responses. Behavior is affected by the character of this circumstance and the essence of the individual.

To learn more and to Bring changes you ought to get in contact.

Classifications Of Human Behavior

Dependent on the way people behave or act in Various scenarios and also in response to stimuli behavior can be broken into various kinds. Let us talk below some significant and famous kinds of behavior.

Listed below are the Kinds of behavior's Human beings may have:

1. Molecular and Moral Behavior

Molecular Behavior: it's an unexpected behavior that happens without believing. If a person is about to the eyes, eyes are closing.

Moller Behavior: Contrary to molecular behavior, this kind of behavior happens after believing. By way of instance, a individual alters how he or she sees that a thing that is damaging.

2. Overt & Covert Behavior

Overt Behavior: it's a visible sort of behavior that could happen out of individual beings. Eating meals, playing soccer, and riding a bike are a few examples.

Covert Behavior: Contrary to overt behavior, This Kind of behavior Is not observable. Believing is a Fantastic example of behavior that is covert because nobody Can view us believing.

3. Voluntary and Involuntary Behavior

Voluntary Behavior: it's a form of behavior that depends upon individual desire. We can describe talking, walking, and writing because of behavior's.

Involuntary Behavior: Contrary to voluntary behavior, this kind happens naturally and without believing. Breathing air is the ideal instance of behavior that is involuntary.

4 Popular Forms of Personalities

A significant research study in human behavior has classified personality into four kinds -- 'optimistic',"pessimistic',"trusting' and 'envious'. Envious is the most frequent type. According to specialists, more than 90 percent of people can be categorized under these classes. There appears to be some balance in various character types.

1. Optimistic:

Approximately 20 percent of those individuals living in this World are thought to have this character. An person keeps trying however difficult circumstances get and stays hopeful. These folks can be bleak in certain scenarios.

2. Pessimistic:

There Appears to Be some balance in distinct Character types. Approximately 20 percent of people of the world have a tendency to own this character. Everything about her or his may be doubted by A person. These folks can be optimistic in certain scenarios.

3. Trusting:

Approximately 20 percent of those individuals living in this World are thought to have this character. Among the traits of individuals that are expecting would be to trust other people. These folks don't require a reason to consider others. There are scenarios when these folks may not trust individuals.

4. Envious:

The Amount of individuals Character changes from society to society. According to research we're currently talking here, about 30 percent of people of the world have a tendency to own this character. Men and women aren't always like that; they could be supportive.

It's important to Mention a single individual might become and, envious trusting. It's a result of the reason that these traits exist in all human beings. As expecting on and the Men and Women That Are able to trust others are known So on.

CREATING VULNERABILITY

When one Gifts Other People React Themselves vulnerable. People connect on a social, individual, and amounts that are animalistic. Vulnerability is hunted to create a relationship. Nobody wants to feel as if they're speaking to a fridge. Vulnerability is in allowing the person know that you're human as 15, essential.

It is reassuring to know there's another Person that is relatable. Most of us have mistaken that are aware, our flaws, and times when we are just lazy. A number people have times when it can be tricky to escape bed. They will be more inclined to get in touch with you if it's possible to show part of the side to another individual. A lot people need to be that person that flawless. We see their hair and skin look at these Instagram stars, and deep down, want we might be like these. Many individuals don't understand they would not wish to be friends with this individual. There has to be an equilibrium when creating connections, therefore presenting yourself as informative will drive away others in the finish.

Is harmful as it becomes codependency. Obviously, it is fantastic to show others who you are a human with feelings and ideas. When seeking to generate a relationship with them however people become determined by others and they wind up dabbling from the world of codependency. When you eliminate your thoughts and feelings and begin to undertake the opinions of other people around you a lot of, there is an opportunity you may have some tendencies that are overburdened.

There are ways a person can present Themselves vulnerable, and they will realize that people respond to this. Sharing is something which may make people uneasy. You do not need to tell your darkest secrets to everybody to create them believe you have a side. There are different methods to prove which you're a person which they can make a relationship with.

- **Request Assistance**

Asking for assistance is a way vulnerability. You are letting the person but you are opting to ask them. You are going out of the way to let them understand they have what it takes to fix your issue. You are giving yet another person responsibility on your own, and that could cause them to feel very strong.

It appears like it might be counterproductive. Why would you wish to show yourself as helpless to some other individual? The secret is not to ask for help. You do not need to place somebody else in an embarrassing scenario where they must do a fantastic favor for you. Just asking for small matters, to borrow something, to connect you as you shop to house sit for a weekend, then these tiny things can help link you to a person you may not otherwise have the ability to relate to.

Another individual, you can join with them on an individual level. You are putting more value in your connection than if you should keep things on a conversational level. You'll see this a lot with the ones that care for kids and educators. They ask the children to do something the children can feel significant, such as they have significance. They could relate to the adults using these tasks that are tiny.

- **Request More**

1 way to Make Certain That you will be able to Convince a person to help is by simply asking for more than you need so as to make certain that you'll at least have half an hour. This is a whole lot to ask of a individual, so there is a chance they will say no. If they do, then you can only ask to borrow their own truck, the principal reason you asked for aid in the first location. They will be more inclined to say yes, since they feel bad about turning your very first petition.

This Is a Great technique Which You Can use In some small business discussions. When placing a deal on a home, you are not likely to provide what you really wish to cover. You will go lower to provide another person a opportunity to cancel back. The exact same type of thinking could be applied to unique interactions and minutes of persuasion with different folks, both on a business and personal level.

You still have to be fair with your requests. You can not expect to utilize this approach to alter a person. If you would like more emotionally from someone, you will not have the ability to request twice as far as everything you require, as everybody has their own pace. This system of persuasion is not applicable in each situation, but it could surely assist you in several distinct conditions.

- **Making Connections**

Assessing and persuading another individual. Nobody wishes to perform favors for somebody they don't have any relationship with. Nobody will have the ability to have a really delighted relationship with a man they don't feel anything for. Some people are more difficult to make connections with. They may have spent a fantastic part of their lives shut, not wanting to meet new men and women. This is frequently because they have been hurt so frequently they don't wish to allow themselves feel pain . They have come to be a different individual that's relied upon themselves and their self for so very long to give happiness. When these folks may be the most difficult to associate with, it is still possible. You need to present yourself vulnerable so as to let them know you don't need to hurt them.

You can not make yourself overly destitute, as Independent folks do not enjoy the ones that appear to be overly reliant on other men and women. It is not simple to find that balance, however it's possible.

Out to make relations. They may feel as though they do not fit in, and nobody knows them. A lot of people are amazed to learn there are in fact many others like those who feel exactly the identical way. Even those who apparently fit in and get along with everybody will discover they still have their moments of isolation.

Occasionally, being a person could be incredibly lonely. You are feeling empty inside along with your own thoughts occasionally, wondering in the event that you can also expect and rely on your own, let alone the people around you. Linking with other individuals may help alleviate these feelings although this sense of isolation might not go away. Letting men and women know they're not alone may allow you to feel connected to other people. There are loads of approaches of getting a relationship but there are, when it comes to meeting new folks.

- **Utilize their Name**

When you make use of their title people today like. It Inform them that you and they're linking. Bosses that may call their workers out by title are more inclined to be respected. However large a corporation how many workers there are or may be, it is almost always a fantastic idea to ensure to understand because people's titles. The specific same ought to be said for the ones which are around. Get acquainted with the individual which makes your coffee at Starbucks, or the title of your mailman.

Some Folks think studying the nametags of It is always much better to wait to inquire their title or to present themselves although Employees can be a means to connect together. Your server may have a nametag on, however instead of calling them out, introduce your self. Should your title is known by them too, people today feel more comfortable if you call them by their own title.

When speaking to folks and having severe Discussions together, it is important to use the name of someone. It allows them know you are speaking about both of you, not merely normally and brings them back. Individuals may recognize because they have spent so long speaking at them rather than to them, their partner isn't called by them by their title.

- **Mirroring Behavior**

After You Can Begin picking up on somebody's Body language, you may begin to comprehend how to mimic their behaviour. Somebody that appears very convinced, constantly standing together with their arms over their heads or using them pointed out in their sides may be more difficult to fit, but it is still important to attempt to mimic this behaviour. Matching confidence is essential in a deal.

You do not need to do so to be To allow them to feel comfortable. A few folks may observe that there is a individual feeling uncomfortable, so they exert their assurance and power and may make the most of the. As you are closing off the chance for them to start up for you, this should not be performed.

If you notice someone is and Shut off, lower your confidence level to coincide. It allows them know they rely on you and can trust you. If a person tapping on their feet from anxiety and is picking in their hands, you do not need to do exactly the same. Just ensure you're in lower or their level, whether so you've got to stand or sit. Keep your arms relaxed leaning your mind to let them know that you are prepared to listen to what they must say and listening. You do not wish to earn anyone feel uneasy than they are.

- **Flattery gets you everywhere**

Sometimes, sucking up to someone can actually work. You don't wish to be inauthentic or around the top with what compliments you're giving to another person, but it is still important to remember precisely how far a little extra love could proceed. There's an opportunity you're already thinking the things that you wish to say anyhow, so why don't you let them how you feel, as long as it is positive.

Flattery doesn't just have to be notification Someone how gorgeous or smart they are. It can be as simple as picking their favorite snack when you are in the store or recalling to ask how their holiday went in case you understand they went away for the weekend. Some individuals could see these items as "kissing ass," or even "brown nosing," but seeking to make a positive connection ought to be a part of our everyday life.

Actually if someone sees what you're doing, They are still oblivious of your conscious attempt to make a connection. It may be quite obvious in some cases that a person is trying to flatter you, especially if they're normally shut off or apparently careless. When some individuals might be bothered by this, many will still enjoy the effort you are putting into attempting to make a relationship with them.

- **The Power of Words**

You, because, free, instantly, and new, these will be the most effective words in the English vocabulary. "You," is an important thing, since people love hearing about themselves. Listen to some 1-3-year-old talk next time you are around them. It might even be the first word most individuals learn!

"Since," is an important word, since Lots of people are looking for an explanation. In a word with so many curiosities and chances, we could feel overwhelmed with how little we know. People are obsessed with tags, and most people like to understand the reason for something. When they hear the word "since," their brain kicks on and become more attentive, awaiting the explanation they are so desperately seeking.

"Free" is a popular term, for a Number of Reasons In our society. On the flip side, it means free stuff! People will spend three hundred bucks on something they don't need whether it means they get one small FREE gift to go along with this. It's possible to genuinely hypnotize someone by using the term "free."

So many folks desire freedom and independence in their lives. The most codependent folks like to hear the phrase "free," even if it's only them getting a illusion of what independence might imply.

"Immediately," is a Excellent word because so A lot of men and women are obsessed with time. All of us have to confront the dark fact: we're going to die 1 day. Even those that are in their 20s still have to know that their days are numbered. We try to fight change as far as you can, but timing is unbeatable, therefore that as we could get more of it, we are hooked, someone promising something instantaneous is going to be popular.

"New," will be the final of the five most popular words. As humans, our brains are wired to continuously look for new expansion. Some folks might be afraid of change, but we still look for new things. "New," reflects growth and life in precisely the exact same time. A few folks might want to wear the same shirt they've needed for years versus a brand new one. However, if provided a new or an old sandwich, then they are going to go for the new one.

These five words Are Extremely important to Include in everybody's terminology, if you are trying to convince a person or not.

What you can do with your body is significant, However, the words that you decide to share are essential as well. It's important to Recall not only with everything you are saying, but with what others are speaking as well. Not everything that is said is exactly what is meant.

Psychological Theories

The Majority of us learned from basic College what there was a scientific concept. It involved the concept of somebody who tests that idea. A psychological concept is comparable, in a psychologist or psychologist thought of something that they found one of their patients, chose to test their concept, then got differing results. There are and the more you understand, the better you will have the ability to analyze somebody else.

A lot is to learn about different Psychology facets so as to understand the psychological theories all science's area has to offer you. Not everybody needs to become psychologist or a therapist to know what some concepts that are distinct may be.

You need to try coming up with your personal as well. You noticed a behavior who you interact with. What's the main cause for them responding this way? How might they respond to a stimulus versus a different group of individuals? Everybody differs, therefore not every concept will apply. It is still interesting to learn how frequently you could be about the predictions that you are making.

If you cannot think of some of your personal Theories to test, we have assembled three which appear to be precise and popular one of the way and also people which you are able to examine those about you. All these are significant theories in creating connections with other individuals, in addition to persuading them if you've got to at a particular scenario.

- **Priming**

You may, if you believe about priming Associate the word with painting. You pick a primer before you choose to paint to place on the walls. This will make sure that the mustard yellow the walls have been painted will not show through because you place a coat of baby blue . In emotional conditions, priming is much like this thought.

This entails setting up discussions and Activities for future prep. This notion is significant in minutes or discussions of persuasion. Priming involves before facing the thing, falling thoughts, pictures, and words to conversations. Priming is used for the ones which are prepared to modify, or people who don't enjoy surprises.

Picture wife and a husband. Perhaps the spouse Wants to have children, but she is convinced her husband is prepared. She understands when confronted; he proceeds to shut off himself and he reacts to change. It took for him to suggest, so she has to be cautious about bringing the baby conversation. She might begin putting on a picture about a kid, priming him. Maybe she will make modest remarks here and there about needing a baby take detours throughout the baby sections in the local department stores. She will need to prime him so once she brings it up, that he does not run and hide.

This Sort of behavior could be manipulative If not employed for the correct reasons. In case the female's husband had said over and over again which he never would alter his mind and didn't want kids, she should not be priming him. There are a number of people who require a drive, and scaring away the husband would not be the means. If somebody is using it for personal profit the way this behaviour would be manipulative is. In case the shift, or what's being primed, will benefit both parties, then it can be a practical instrument to be able to get exactly what you would like.

- **Amplification Hypothesis**

The amplification theory is Involves surrounding a topic that is specific or heightening the excitement. A lot of individuals use this form of procedure before realizing they are currently doing. The procedure involves taking a topic, thing, or alternative notion, and essentially gassing up it, which makes it appear more thrilling, and amplifying it to another level. This entails speaking down something so as to change viewpoints, or building this up.

Let us look at wife and your husband out of the Last segment. She might choose to utilize this procedure by talking about how infants that are good are. She'll come home and go over her friends' infant and perfect and how adorable it was. She will not mention rather and that she has puke on her top only discuss the cute sounds and faces the infant. If that is the way he feels, Alternately, his hatred might be amplified by the husband for kids. Maybe he will point out a crying infant when they are in public, stating things like,"thank God we do not have children."

The amplification theory is To utilize it, although Accurate is the best choice. It's much better to be honest about the feelings and have the standard conversation without meanings that are concealed. This sort of procedure may be great as they would like. When working on jobs in business or in your private life, if you are working with other people, there will be. The amplification procedure is able to help you reveal your feelings without saying or breaking down the thought of somebody else.

- **The Scarcity Effect**

The effect is that if There's less of something, it could be desirable. This is considered in earnings. Consider the shop you moved to. There were probably commercials that said things such as, "just two weeks left, "while supplies last," or "limited period " The majority of the time, this is not accurate whatsoever and are utilized for folks to purchase faster. This impact functions which is the reason why it is still used by so many companies. The identical sort of impact can be earned in relationships and discussions. When seeking to convince a person, restricting availability or the time of a choice can help influence them faster.

Playing hard for can help. While it's Important so as to create connections to reveal exposure, in addition, it is important to keep a certain space. There is a notion that some folks like"bad boys," and this is regarding the scarcity effect. The thought that you can not have something makes folks want it more. The fear could be what compels a individual.

If there are just two One totally filled and one having four or three biscuits, jars left most will select the jar that empty. Most will presume that the jar that empty has biscuits that are greater tasting cutter, although they might be the exact same sort of cookie. People place their time and effort into eating the biscuits that are other, so that they have something better.

WHAT'S A PERSONALITY TYPE?

Kind refers to the Classification of people of different kinds. Types are distinguished from character traits, together with the latter embodying a group of trends. Whereas traits may be categorized as differences types are believed to demand differences between individuals. What makes? Every individual has an notion of their personality type -- whenever they're booked or bubbly, thick-skinned or sensitive. Psychologists who attempt to tease out the science of that we're currently defining character have a tendency to believe, feel and act.

There are many ways but psychologists have given up on attempting neatly. They concentrate on character traits.

5 Traits

1. Openness
2. Conscientiousness
3. Extraversion
4. Agreeableness
5. Neuroticism

Conveniently, these traits can be remembered by you Using the convenient OCEAN mnemonic (or, should you would rather, CANOE functions, also).

The Big Five were created in the 1970s by Two research groups. The Big Five are Up each person's character. Someone may have no neuroticism, a great deal of conscientiousness, an quantity of extraversion, a lot of agreeableness and a dash of openness. Or somebody could be conscientious, neurotic, introverted, unpleasant and open. Here Is What each attribute involves:

Openness

experience." Love experience. They love art, creativity and new items and're curious. The motto of this open person could be "Variety is the spice of life"

Individuals are the Reverse: avoid adventures that are new, they like to follow their customs and likely are not the adventurous eaters. Changing personality is regarded as a process that was challenging, but openness is. The effect lasted a year.

Talking of drug use that is experimental, California's Civilization that is try-anything isn't a myth. An analysis of personality traits across the United States discovered that openness is the most prevalent on the West Coast.

Conscientiousness

Are coordinated and possess a sense of obligation. They are disciplined, reliable and achievement-focused. Types jetting off with a backpack journeys won't be found by you.

Individuals are somewhat more Spontaneous and freewheeling. They might tend toward carelessness. Conscientiousness is a attribute as it's been associated with success in college and at work.

Extraversion

Maybe the Big Five's most character trait. An someone's more is, the more of a butterfly they're. Extraverts are social, chatty and draw energy out of audiences. They are inclined to be merry and assertive.

Introverts

Time, perhaps their brains procedure interaction. Both are not the same, although introversion is frequently confused with shyness. Shyness suggests that a fear of an inability or social interactions to function. Introverts can be charming at celebrations -- they like small-group or solo pursuits.

Agreeableness

Agreeableness steps the extent of a Individual's tranquility and warmth. The individual that is pleasant is, the more inclined they are to be more helpful, expecting and compassionate. Men and women are suspicious and cold and they are not as inclined to collaborate. Are Judged to be listeners by girls, indicating that character can be signaled by body motion. (Conscientiousness also makes for great dancers, based on the exact same 2011 study.) But at the office, more than fine men are really earned by unpleasant men. Girls that are disagreeable did not demonstrate exactly the salary edge, suggesting a demeanor is beneficial to guys.

Getting Being considered not agreeable, was proven to be the most frequent character type from the four research with a report published from the journal in August 2016 Science Advances. Men and women feel if somebody else is more effective than they are threatened.

Neuroticism

To know neuroticism, look no farther Compared to George Costanza of those long-running sitcom "Seinfeld." George is famed because of his neuroses, which the series blames on his parents. He obsesses over disease and germs worries about what and quits a project because his fear over not having access to some toilet is overpowering.

George could be elevated on the neuroticism Scale; however, the character trait is actual. Individuals slip into depression and anxiety and high in neuroticism anxiety. Neurotic men and women tend to seek out things to be worried about if all is going well. One study discovered that when individuals with wages earned earnings, the income made them happy.

Neuroticism tend to be even-keeled and secure.

Neuroticism is linked with Lots of health outcomes. Men and women die younger than the secure since they flip into alcohol and tobacco to ease their nerves.

Probably the most creepy truth about Neuroticism is that parasite can cause you to believe like that. And we are not speaking. Disease by the parasite Toxoplasma gondii can make individuals vulnerable to neuroticism, a 2006 research found.

Instinct and sensing refer to individuals Prefer to collect information about the Earth, if through concrete info (sensing) or psychological feelings (instinct). Sense and thinking refer to the way decisions are made by folks. Thinking kinds go with logic, whilst their hearts are followed by feeling forms.

The judging/perception dichotomy, which explains how folks decide to interact with the entire world. Judging types like actions that is critical, while perceiving types favor choices that are open. The machine further defines 16 personality types according to a combination of four of those groups, resulting in descriptions like ISTP, ENFP, ESFJ, etc.

4 Personality Types

Employing the traits Researchers measured that the poll results to discover 4 personality clusters.

Average

Most personality type that is Frequent

High in neuroticism and extraversion - tending to be more sociable, assertive, pessimistic, and over-sensitive

Low in openness - tending to be more routine-based and less open to abstraction

Tend to seek attention, but are not overly intellectually curious

More likely to be female, than male

Reserved

Nations of agreeableness and Conscientiousness - tending to become trusting, sensitive, well-known, and trustworthy

Lower openness and neuroticism - tending to stay the course with confidence

Emotionally stable

Somewhat not so, although extraverted

Role Models

High in extraversion Agreeableness, and conscientiousness - tending to display qualities which elicit respect and admired direction

Confident and courageous, taking calculated risks

Reputable and receptive to new ideas

Strong leaders

Likelihood for a part model increases with age

Self-Centered

High in extraversion - must be quite

Saturated in conscientiousness, agreeableness, and openness - tending

In the cost of Other people

Likelihood to be decreases with age

Recognizing ourselves and our coworkers is Crucial to nurturing relationships on the job and in home. Personalities are a spectrum, and also a label that is clustered should define who we are.

What's most Important is to realize that the world is approached by every one of those . How we perceive every impacts our activities and the world. A number of those senses may be more useful than others To recognize that which traits assist versus harm.

Can Personality Change?

More importantly, personalities Aren't static--they can and do change over time. This demonstrates that we are always continuously learning, and that our life adventures will continue to shape how we perceive and interact with our world. Personality could be changed through treatment. "For the men and women who wish to modify their spouse tomorrow, that a good deal of people want to do, I do not have much hope for these," said study researcher Brent Roberts, a social and personality psychologist in the University of Illinois. But he continued, "if you are eager to focus on a single element of yourself, and you're willing to go at it systematically, there's now raised optimism which you are able to impact change in that domain name."

Myers & Briggs' 16 Personality Types

Have you ever heard someone explain Themselves as an INTJ or a ESTP and wondered what these cryptic-sounding letters may mean? These folks are speaking to is that their personality type dependent on the Myers-Briggs Type Indicator (MBTI).

Is a self-report stock made to identify a individual's personality style, strengths, and preferences. The poll was designed by Isabel Myers and her mother Katherine Briggs based on their job with Carl Jung's theory of personality types.

The Development of this Myers-Briggs Test

Were thinking with Jung's theory of psychological types and also understood that the theory might have real-world software. Throughout World War II, both Myers and Briggs started investigating and developing an indicator that may be used to help understand different differences. By helping people know themselves, Myers and Briggs believed they might help people select occupations that were suitable to their own character styles and lead healthier, happier lives.

Myers created the first pen-and-pencil Variant of this stock throughout the 1940s, and the two girls started testing the evaluation on friends and family. They continued to fully develop the tool over the subsequent two decades.

A Summary of the Test

Depending on the replies to the questions on The stock, people are recognized as using one of 16 personality types. The objective of the MBTI is to permit researchers to further research and understand their particular personalities including their own likes, dislikes, strengths, weaknesses, possible career tastes, and compatibility with different people.

No one personality type is "greatest" Or "better" than any other person. It isn't an instrument designed to search for dysfunction or abnormality. Rather, its objective is just to help you understand more about yourself.

The questionnaire itself Is Composed of four Different scales:

Extraversion (E) - Introversion (I)

The extraversion-introversion dichotomy has been First explored by Jung in his concept of personality types as a means to clarify how people react and interact with the world around them. While certain terms are familiar to most people, the manner by which they are employed here differs somewhat in their popular use.

Extraverts (also frequently spelled extroverts) are "outward-turning" and also are inclined to be action-oriented, love more regular social interaction, also feel energized after spending some time with different people.

Introverts are all "inward-turning" and tend to be thought-oriented and enjoy profound and significant social interactions, and texture recharged after spending some time alone. Most of us show extraversion and introversion to a degree, but most of us have an overall preference for one or the other.

Sensing (S) – Intuition (N)

This scale entails looking at how individuals Collect information from the world about them. The same as with extraversion and introversion, all people spend some time sensing and intuiting based on the circumstance. According to the MBTI, individuals tend be dominant in one place or another. People who prefer sensing tend to pay a good deal of attention to fact, particularly to that which they could learn from their own senses. They have a tendency to focus on details and facts and enjoy getting hands-on expertise. People who prefer intuition pay more attention to things like patterns and impressions. They enjoy considering chances, imagining the future, and abstract theories.

Thinking (T) – Feeling (F)

This scale focuses on the way Folks make Decisions based on the information that they gathered in their instinct or sensing functions. People who favor thinking place a larger emphasis on facts and objective information. They tend to be consistent, plausible, and unbiased when contemplating a decision. Those to favor setting are more likely to think about people and emotions when arriving at a conclusion.

Judging (J) - Perceiving (P)

The Last scale entails how people tend to Deal with the external world. People who lean toward judging prefer structure and company decisions. Individuals who lean toward perceiving are somewhat more spacious, flexible, and elastic. These two tendencies interact with all the other scales. Keep in mind, all people at least spend a while extroverting. The judging-perceiving scale aids explain whether you extravert whenever you are taking in new information (sensing and intuiting) or whenever you are making decisions (thinking and feeling).

Each type is then listed by its own four-letter code:

ISTJ - The Inspector

ISTJs are accountable organizers, driven to Make and enforce order within systems and institutions. They're tidy and neat, inside and out, and tend to get a process of everything they do.

ISTP - The Crafter

ISTPs are observant people with an Understanding of mechanics and also an interest in troubleshooting. They approach their surroundings using a elastic logic, searching for practical solutions to the issues at hand.

ISFJ - The Counselor

INFJs are imaginative nurturers using a powerful Awareness of personal ethics and a drive to help others realize their potential. Creative and committed, they've a talent for helping others with initial solutions to their own challenges.

ISFP - The Composer

ISFPs are mild caretakers who live in the Present moment and revel in their surroundings with merry, low-key excitement. They're spontaneous and flexible, and like to go with the flow to enjoy what life has to offer you.

INFJ - The Counselor

INFJs are imaginative nurturers using a powerful Awareness of personal integrity and also a push to help others understand their potential. Creative and dedicated, they have a knack for helping others with all initial solutions to their personal challenges.

INFP - The Healer

INFPs are imaginative idealists, guided by Their own core values and beliefs. To some Healer, chances are predominant; the fact of this moment is just of death concern. They see potential for a much better future, and pursue truth and significance with their own flair.

INTJ - The Mastermind

INTJs are analytic problem-solvers, excited To enhance systems and processes with their revolutionary ideas.

They've a knack for viewing chances for advancement, whether at work, in your home, or in themselves.

Fascinated by logical analysis, strategies, and design. They are obsessed with theory, and hunt for your universal law supporting everything they see. They wish to understand the unifying themes of life, in all their elegance.

ESTP - The Dynamo

ESTPs are lively thrill seekers that are In their best when putting out flames, whether or not metaphorical. They bring a feeling of lively energy for their own interactions with other people and the world around them.

ESTJ - The Supervisor

Keen to participate in organizing projects and people. Orderly, rule-abiding, and diligent, ESTJs prefer to get things done, and have a tendency to go about projects in a systematic, methodical way.

ESFP - The Performer

ESFPs are lively entertainers who appeal And engage those around them. They're spontaneous, energetic, and fun-loving, and enjoy the things about them: food, clothing, nature, creatures, and especially individuals.

ESFJ - The Provider

ESFJs are conscientious helpers, sensitive To the needs of other people and energetically devoted to their own responsibilities. They are highly attuned to their own psychological surroundings and attentive to the feelings of other people and the perception others have of these.

ENFP - The Champion

ENFPs are people-centered founders with a Concentrate on chances and a contagious enthusiasm for new ideas, individuals and activities. Energetic, warm, and enthusiastic, ENFPs really like to help other men and women explore their creative potential.

ENFJ - The Teacher

ENFJs have been idealist organizers, pushed to Implement their vision of what is ideal for humanity. They often act as catalysts for individual growth due to their ability to determine potential in different people and their fascination in alerting others to their thoughts.

ENTP - The Visionary

ENTPs are motivated innovators, moved to Find new answers to challenging issues. They're curious and clever, and seek to understand the individuals, strategies, and fundamentals which encircle them.

ENTJ - The Commander

ENTJs are strategic leaders, motivated to Arrange alter. They are fast to view inefficiency and conceptualize new alternatives, and enjoy developing long-lived plans to accomplish their vision. They excel at logical reasoning and are generally contested and quick-witted.

The Largest Weakness of Every Myers-Briggs Personality Type

Each of us has weak places, and while others Of these probably have nothing to do with character type, a few probably will! When it comes to personality type, every one of us comes with a range of purposes, and while particular functions have a tendency to be (but aren't always) more conscious and healthier, other purposes have a tendency to be weaker and more unconscious. In most cases we rely mainly on our dominant function, support that function together with our auxiliary function, find aid with our tertiary purpose, and also our weak spot is our inferior function.

Usually at least one of our flaws Stems from unhealthy growth or suppression of the poor function. If we spend all our time disregarding input from our inferior function we can overwork our dominant role and fall "to the grip" of our inferior function. While this happens, we become stressed, ridiculous, and anxious. Proper, balanced evolution of the poor function can assist individuals to have a more balanced perspective, be more understanding of people different from us, and can enable individuals to experience less anxiety in our lives.

The Weak Spot of Each Myers-Briggs Personality Form The Introverted Sensing Personality Types: ISTJ and ISFJ

ISTJs and ISFJs have inferior Extraverted Intuition (Ne). This usually means that they would rather concentrate on realistic, practical realities than theoretical or abstract possibilities. Their focus is much more on the real, tangible world compared to the world of everything "may be" or "what if's". They prefer to trust methods and may shirk from untested strategies. When they plan that they prefer to look at what has worked and use those exact approaches in the future. ISJs who invest just a tiny bit of time every day working on the maturation of Ne can experience immense personal growth. This tends to be simpler since they enter later life, as most of kinds naturally are inclined to operate on developing the inferior function at the point. But regardless of where you're in life, there are a number of excellent strategies to market healthier extraverted intuition.

It is Necessary to Keep in Mind that you should Only practice those techniques in times of reduced stress. If you're worried, focusing on your inferior function can simply cause you to feel more stressed and nervous.

Techniques To Develop Extraverted Intuition:

-- Start noticing patterns in your lifetime. Do You see any patterns in how you interact with people or the world around you? Can you observe any unusual relationships or patterns involving the folks you enjoy and the items they use?

Just had one day left to live? What could you do otherwise? Are there any patterns or bad habits you wish you could have avoided? How would you wish you'd spent your own time?

-- Think about a problem you're now experiencing. List ten potential solutions. The problem can be little (the best way to get an additional fifteen minutes of sleep in the morning) or large (how to manage a terrible connection).

-- Can there be a location you'd like to Go to Someday that you've never been to? Is there a project you would love to do someday that you've never completed? How could you merge these two life objects and make them a reality? Is there more than one way you might do so?

-- Once a day attempt to stop yourself before Do it. Ask yourself whether you have considered any alternative possibilities or alternatives that might be an enhancement.

-- Think about something damaging that bugs you. How could you turn into a positive? Is there some good lesson to be learned by this?

-- Try something fresh in your routine; Whether it is a new hairdo, a new genre of movie, a new color of lipstick, or a new recipe!

The Extraverted Sensing Personality Types: Estp And Esfp

ESTPs and ESFPs have lower Introverted Intuition (Ni). They fancy the world of current realities to the world of "may be" and "will bee's". They would rather focus more on now compared to distant future. Practical, real world realities they can see, smell, touch, and taste are far more appealing and exciting compared to theoretical possibilities and respectful, subjective imaginings. ESPs that spend just a little time every day working on the development of Introverted Intuition may have stronger instincts, better tactical planning abilities, and also make wiser long-term decisions. ESPs obviously begin to come up with Ni in later life, particularly in their 50s and 60s. But, any ESP may find a head-start at developing Ni if they set their mind to it!

It's Important to Keep in Mind that you should Only practice those methods in times of reduced stress. If you are worried, focusing in your poor function can simply cause you to feel more anxious and stressed.

Ways to Develop Introverted Intuition:

-- Write down random ideas and "visions" That pop into your head from the blue. Draw a picture of them if you'd prefer.

-- invest Some Time in quiet Contemplation or meditation each day.

-- Envision your life as a movie or a novel. How would that film or novel perform? Would you be the hero or the villain? How would you want to have that book or film to end?

-- Think of someone who you know. Write a list Of their negative qualities. Now rewrite the same list with a favorable interpretation of those same attributes. It may be hard, but see if you can come up with another perspective on each quality you recorded! Do some images pop in your mind as you're doing this?

--"Zoom out" your lifetime. Consider a Problem you're presently experiencing and imagine how everyone is affected or finds that same issue. How can your mother see it? How does your very best buddy see it? How can your enemy see it? Write down every perspective and see if an image or emblem comes to head that synthesizes most of the viewpoints united.

-- Envision that your life in ten years. What Pictures do you see? What possibilities do you detect? What seems likely or unlikely?

-- After watching a film or reading a book, Reflect on just what the story intended to you or represented.

-- Pick up a magazine and look at the Advertisements. What's the real intention behind these words? What will be the advertisers hoping to "sell" you? Is it true or are they currently being fallacious? What are they manipulating the audience? Are you currently employing any symbols or colors to influence people?

The Introverted Intuitive Personality Types: INTJs and INFJs

INTJs and INFJs have inferior Extraverted They like to focus on the abstract world of unconscious fantasies and possibilities over the practical, real world they could see, smell, touch and taste. They are inclined to tinker with thoughts, views, and theoretical possibilities in their heads and they're pulled towards a vision they feel their life should be. They have a tendency to look down to "living in the moment" and want to concentrate on the long run. They may eliminate sight of current realities and specifics as they toy with thoughts in their minds. They can get so focused on what "will likely be" they lose sight of what's needed at this time. It's important for INJs to devote a little time every day developing Se so that they can experience better personal growth and enjoy life more completely.

It's Important to Keep in Mind that you should Only practice these methods in times of reduced stress. If you are worried, focusing in your inferior function can only make you feel more stressed and nervous.

Ways to Develop Extraverted Sensing:

-- Perform the blindfold game. Have a friend Blindfold you and hand you something to smell, touch, or taste. Concentrate on tasting, feeling, or smelling the product fully and providing that experience your full attention. Initially don't be concerned about imagining what the item is, simply worry about taking in the feeling and remaining in the present time.

-- Look about you. Does anything excite Your senses? Can there be a candle you may light? A food you could taste? A spice you could experiment with? A person you may hug? How could you adopt the moment you're in and encounter something concrete at this time?

-- Look at a piece of artwork for fifteen seconds. Now turn away and try to generate a listing of every specific detail you recall. Don't write exactly what the details symbolize, simply write what they are.

-- Eat slowly. Savor each flavor and attempt to Enjoy it entirely.

-- Do something practical to help somebody; Cook them a meal pull weeds for them, shovel their snow.

-- Attempt to learn a new game like tennis, Soccer, or even dance! Attempt to stay in the present time and pay close attention to what's happening around you.

-- Try a new outdoor recreational activity. Move white-water holiday, hiking, or even skydiving!

-- Think of a concrete problem You're facing. How do you solve that issue using real resources already at your disposal?

-- Take a stroll and notice the fine details Of everything about you. Bring a camera and try zooming in on parts of character as much as you can.

The Extraverted Intuitive Personality Groups: ENTPs and ENFPs

ENTPs and ENFPs have poor Introverted Because of this, they are inclined to prefer new possibilities and theoretical inventions over "tried and true" techniques or patterns. They can grow to be so centered on the long run and what "could" occur that they neglect to notice what they want today. This can result in them needing to eat, fearing to sleep sufficient, or missing present details which are important. Where sensors are at risk of never seeing the forest for the trees, even intuitive are in danger of not even seeing the trees to the forest. ENPs working on growing Si may be more aware, more physically fit, and much better able to pay attention to details which are essential for their daily life. All types tend to improve their inferior function in later life, but there is no reason that you cannot start sooner than that!

It's Important to Keep in Mind that you ought to Only practice those techniques in times of reduced stress. If you are stressed, focusing on your poor function can just make you feel more anxious and stressed.

Ways to Develop Introverted Sensing:

-- Have a moment to reflect how you feel In detail at this time. Just how do you feel physically? Are you tense relaxed or everywhere? Are you hungry or tired? How do you feel emotionally? Are you anxious, happy, unhappy? Take moments during the day to check in with yourself and actually understand what is happening within your body and mind.

-- Next time the brainstorming, visit how Many solutions it is possible to come across that are successful in the past.

-- Think about a favorite memory. Where were you? What did you feel like? Are there some sights, sounds, or smells that you can recall? Close your eyes and try to cover yourself from the memory.

-- Tell a story in consecutive order. Start In the start and make sure you don't bounce about in time.

-- Understand Precisely What you did that made Someone happy before. Do exactly the identical thing again.

-- Take up a hobby such as knitting, Pay attention to how the rep involved can make you feel relaxed.

-- Think about your daily routine (in case you Have one). Is there anything you might do to add more consistency into your regular and so less anxiety?

perfume. What exactly does the odor remind you? What do you encounter or think about?

The Introverted Thinking Personality Types: INTP and ISTP

INTPs and ISTPs have lower Extraverted Feeling (Fe) as well Consequently, may struggle with being aware of other people's Values and feelings. They are extremely analytical and logical and fancy the World of motive to the world of opinions. They're attracted into the world of their Mind at the place where they can categorize and sort out thoughts by their principles and Core truths. When it comes to the universe of emotions and understanding how other Folks feel, ITPs could be a small confused or lost. They tend to suppress this. Function and as a result, they might struggle with social connections and Understanding appropriate behavior. They Might Have difficulty becoming tactful or Understanding other people's psychological states and responding in a means that's understanding. ITPs who create Fe can have stronger relationships, texture more Confident socially, and may also become more connected with their own values It's important to remember that you should only practice these techniques in times of low stress. If you are stressed, focusing in your poor function can simply Make you feel more anxious and stressed.

Ways to Develop Extraverted Feeling:

Other men and women. Notice the way they socialize and attempt to pick up on some suggestions that would reveal how particular individuals feel. Can you observe some social habits which people are demonstrating? Does anybody appear to be concealing any special emotions?

-- Consider those people in your lifetime that have Helped you and harm you. What principles did they promote or offend? Notice exactly what your values are because you do that exercise.

-- Speak to individuals who have distinct values Out of your own. Request them (tactfully) regarding these and when they would be prepared to share the reason why they think and appreciate those items.

-- E-mail somebody you care for or compose Them a letter to inquire how they are doing!

-- Bring snacks or coffee to your co-workers. Learn which sort of coffee they enjoy or what type of snacks they like. Try to consider that.

-- Can you notice anybody in your Loved Ones or Office who looks excluded? Why is it that they look excluded? Is there anything that you can do in order to promote them make their day ?

-- listen to audio (with singing). Attempt to Identify the feelings the singer is atmosphere in detail

-- On your household consider everything you might be Performing to create your spouse's life simpler. Have they exhibited some non-verbal cues about the things they want or want? What principles are you currently in your children? Are these the principles that you would like to instill in these?

ENTJs and ESTJs have poor Introverted Because of this, they have a tendency to prefer the area of logic and intent info over the sphere of private values and significance. They are sometimes so concentrated on actions and getting things done they touch base with everything they believe is wrong or right or what they are affecting them mentally. They could battle with understanding others emotions and needs in their attempts to be successful or purely aim. ETJs who build Fi are somewhat aware of how they believe and that which constitutes up with their worth, they could be more educated with different men and women, and they're able to get a deeper comprehension of their dignity and individual morals. The poor function obviously will grow in daily life, however ETJs of any era can devote some time every day working on creating it.

It is Important to Not Forget that focusing on Your poor role during times of rather extreme anxiety can cause you to feel more stressed and stressed. Attempt to exercise these items through a period of reduced stress.

Tactics to Create Introverted Feeling:

-- What can you care about? What Worth have you ever caught yourself aggressively defending? Consider why these values are very important for you and write down your reasons.

-- Once you see a film or read a novel and You notice something terrible happen to somebody else, imagine how that might feel if it had been you. Attempt to go through the feelings and emotions which the character may be having and attempt to empathize entirely.

To your feelings. What do you really believe that they're attempting to inform you? Can there be a value of yours included? Does one sense "right" or even "incorrect"?

-- Create a list of your values and beliefs. Which ones do you stick to if everybody you loved did not share them?

-- Next time somebody does something which Goes against your own beliefs or beliefs, have a little time to think the way you're able to take care of the problem with ethics.

-- Every time you decided, pause and Consider if that decision complies with your values and can be consistent with your integrity.

-- When Folks speak with you or discuss their issues Together with you, cease and actively pay attention.

Attempt to place any discussions or other ideas from mind. Do not attempt to invent your answer to them whenever they are talking. Simply listen to your whole attention.

-- Locate a reason that interferes with your values. Do you really care about the homeless? About the surroundings? Creatures? Locate a means to volunteer to assist these triggers.

The Introverted Feeling Personality Forms: INFPs and ISFPs

INFPs and ISFPs have poor Extraverted Because of this, they prefer the sphere of subjective worth and significance over the sphere of purpose logic and information. They may eliminate sight of motive when they become chilled in their own feelings, or else they might struggle with becoming as effective and effective as they would like to be. They can struggle with receiving or giving objective criticism since they're concerned about the way other men and women believe or they simply take things. IFPs who create Te may be productive, rational, and manage criticism (and provide it) more easily and efficiently. The poor function obviously develops in after life, however IFPs of any era can shell out a couple of minutes daily strengthening and developing this purpose.

It is Important to Not Forget that focusing on Your poor role during times of rather extreme anxiety can cause you to feel more stressed and nervous. Attempt to exercise these items through a period of reduced stress.

Tactics to Produce Extraverted Thinking:

-- Consider all of the actions That You're Doing this are not vital to achieve your targets. Are there some which you're able to spend less time?

-- Think about a goal You've Got and split it Down to bite-sized measures. By way of instance, "I wish to write a novel". Create a list beginning with "Compose an outline to your book".

-- Produce a plan for the day which focuses On your important objectives and requirements. Consider the way you are able to structure your daily life to satisfy your own targets but also satisfy your own personal requirements.

Say exactly what you Want without being fearful. Say what has to be achieved without feeling as if you are being "bossy".

-- Request for constructive criticism from Somebody you trust. Practice carrying the criticism impersonally and also. Is your criticism true? In what ways will the criticism help you be positive shift? Communicate your ideas to the individual who gave the criticism.

-- Plan a discussion with someone you adore and trust. Locate a place of debate that is not exceptionally personal (you do not wish to hurt your connection). Attempt to acquire the discussion with pure logic. Work on persuasive your buddy of the signs of your promises. Locate inconsistencies within their sense and tip them out.

-- Reorganize a tiny area of Your House, Office, or automobile.

-- Find a way to make the Usual chore more efficient. Can there be a way you can work out and spend some time with your children concurrently? Can there be a way that your laundry-routine can be more effective?

The Extraverted Feeling Personality Forms: ENFJs and ESFJs

ENFJs and ESFJs have poor Introverted Because of this, they'd rather concentrate on their worth and the stability of the others than impartial logic and investigation. They've a fine-tuned comprehension of different people and the way they feel and think, but they are able to battle with focusing on pure factual information and making conclusions which are based on rational pros and cons rather than personal wants and stability. EFJs who build Ti may be balanced, effective, and sensible in their own conclusions. They could feel fuller and turned with the requirements of different people and much more capable of making objective, logical conclusions. The poor function obviously will grow into later life, however EFJs of any era can begin developing this role in their everyday life.

It is Important to Not Forget that focusing on Your poor role during times of rather extreme anxiety can cause you to feel more stressed and nervous. Attempt to exercise these items through a period of reduced stress.

Tactics to Create Introverted Thinking:

-- Create a record of your enemies, friends, And family . Now kind that list into groups that are different and do not overlap with one another.

-- Find out a strategy game and consider the Underlying function and construction of this game. Pre-determine your motions and think about how they are going to perform.

-- Compose a story about something you are Interested in. Use as exact language as you can. Read your own report and eliminate any extraneous terminology or words that are unnecessary. Continue making the record as exact and honest as you can. Think of alternative words (or use a thesaurus) to compose with as clear and precise an objective as you possibly can.

-- For a single day clinic answering questions With just what you had been requested. Do not put anything. By way of instance, whenever someone asks you how you're doing, it is possible to say "I am exhausted " Do not add "I am tired. It has been a very long moment. I had been X up at night and nearly missed my alarm!"

-- Think about ways you can categorize your Recipes, your filing cabinet, or even your own books. Re-organize employing these classes.

-- Consider your fundamentals. What are Some myths which you stick to in each portion of your daily life? So what principles do you always live by?

-- Think about all of the people that you know. If You'd just one day left to live, that can you prioritize viewing and spending some time with?

-- If you are listening to somebody speak, Notice their fundamentals. What truths do they really grip to regardless of what? What groups do they use to support their own arguments? Are you currently equating things from various categories? Are there any defects in his or her argument?

CONCLUSION

This publication must have provided you with a Standard comprehension of how to test and convince those about you. While each person is special in their own manner, there are surely things which are alike between each person. The majority of us have a desire to satisfy our personal needs and desires, and if these ideas are accomplished, the man or woman can be analyzed. The way the person was increased and also the environment they grew up is quite vital in deciding exactly what it is that makes a individual unique.

When assessing a different Individual, it begins with studying their body language. Can they maintain themselves do they hide beneath their very own body? The way someone uses their eyes, head, and arms would be the most crucial sections of deciding what they may really look like. It's possible for you to understand that somebody who looks confident may really be daunted by their nervousness if you begin to observe how that they hold themselves. You can also find that a person you thought you can expect is really tricking you.

It can be Difficult to pinpoint exactly what it's all about A individual who divides them from other people, and the reason why they may behave the way that they do. You are never going to have a comprehensive comprehension of some other individual, but you'll be in a position to begin to understand the reason why they may behave the way that they do.

As Soon as You've managed to analyze somebody, It is possible to then begin to convince them. This can be essential in some instances to get exactly what you would like, or at the least, get exactly what you deserve. As we discussed in publication, you may read that over and above, but if you don't do it, nothing will change. It can be tough to begin to become conscious of your self, but it is an integral step in becoming conscious of those about you.

As Soon as You have the ability to test Yourself and the others, you will be in a position to persuade and convince them well. When you can do this, you'll understand All of the power You've Got on your life.